1-11-00
CH

LOUIS FARRAKHAN

Therese De Angelis

CHELSEA HOUSE PUBLISHERS
Philadelphia

Chelsea House Publishers

Editor in Chief	Stephen Reginald
Managing Editor	James D. Gallagher
Production Manager	Pamela Loos
Art Director	Sara Davis
Photo Editor	Judy L. Hasday
Senior Production Editor	Lisa Chippendale

Staff for LOUIS FARRAKHAN

Senior Editor	John Ziff
Associate Art Director	Takeshi Takahashi
Picture Researcher	Gillian Speeth
Cover Illustrator	Earl Parker

First Printing

1 3 5 7 9 8 6 4 2

Library of Congress Cataloging-in-Publication Data

De Angelis, Therese.
Louis Farrakhan / Therese De Angelis.
    p.   cm. — (Black Americans of Achievement)

Summary: A biography of the Afro-American who dreamed of a career as a violinist before joining the Nation of Islam and rising in its ranks, eventually becoming its leader.

ISBN 0-7910-4688-5 (hardcover)
ISBN 0-7910-4689-3 (pbk.)

1. Farrakhan, Louis—Juvenile literature. 2. Black Muslims—Biography—Juvenile literature. [1. Farrakhan, Louis. 2. Black Muslims. 3. Afro-Americans—Biography.] I. Title. II. Series.
BP223.Z8F382 1998
297.8'7—dc21
[B]   98-6101
                                        CIP
                                        AC

CONTENTS

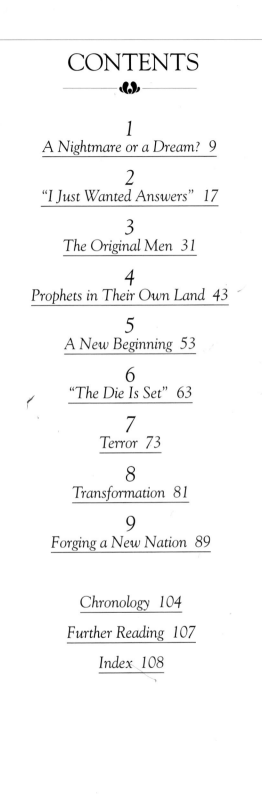

BLACK AMERICANS OF ACHIEVEMENT

HENRY AARON
baseball great

KAREEM ABDUL-JABBAR
basketball great

MUHAMMAD ALI
heavyweight champion

RICHARD ALLEN
*religious leader and
social activist*

MAYA ANGELOU
author

LOUIS ARMSTRONG
musician

ARTHUR ASHE
tennis great

JOSEPHINE BAKER
entertainer

JAMES BALDWIN
author

BENJAMIN BANNEKER
scientist and mathematician

AMIRI BARAKA
poet and playwright

COUNT BASIE
bandleader and composer

ROMARE BEARDEN
artist

JAMES BECKWOURTH
frontiersman

MARY MCLEOD BETHUNE
educator

GEORGE WASHINGTON
CARVER
botanist

CHARLES CHESNUTT
author

BILL COSBY
entertainer

PAUL CUFFE
merchant and abolitionist

MILES DAVIS
musician

FATHER DIVINE
religious leader

FREDERICK DOUGLASS
abolitionist editor

CHARLES DREW
physician

W. E. B. DU BOIS
scholar and activist

PAUL LAURENCE DUNBAR
poet

DUKE ELLINGTON
bandleader and composer

RALPH ELLISON
author

JULIUS ERVING
basketball great

LOUIS FARRAKHAN
political activist

ELLA FITZGERALD
singer

MARCUS GARVEY
black nationalist leader

JOSH GIBSON
baseball great

WHOOPI GOLDBERG
entertainer

ALEX HALEY
author

PRINCE HALL
social reformer

JIMI HENDRIX
musician

MATTHEW HENSON
explorer

BILLIE HOLIDAY
singer

LENA HORNE
entertainer

WHITNEY HOUSTON
singer and actress

LANGSTON HUGHES
poet

ZORA NEALE HURSTON
author

JESSE JACKSON
civil-rights leader and politician

MICHAEL JACKSON
entertainer

JACK JOHNSON
heavyweight champion

MAGIC JOHNSON
basketball great

SCOTT JOPLIN
composer

BARBARA JORDAN
politician

MICHAEL JORDAN
basketball great

CORETTA SCOTT KING
civil-rights leader

MARTIN LUTHER KING, JR.
civil-rights leader

LEWIS LATIMER
scientist

SPIKE LEE
filmmaker

CARL LEWIS
champion athlete

JOE LOUIS
heavyweight champion

RONALD MCNAIR
astronaut

MALCOLM X
militant black leader

BOB MARLEY
musician

THURGOOD MARSHALL
Supreme Court justice

TONI MORRISON
author

ELIJAH MUHAMMAD
religious leader

EDDIE MURPHY
entertainer

JESSE OWENS
champion athlete

SATCHEL PAIGE
baseball great

CHARLIE PARKER
musician

ROSA PARKS
civil-rights leader

COLIN POWELL
military leader

PAUL ROBESON
singer and actor

JACKIE ROBINSON
baseball great

DIANA ROSS
entertainer

WILL SMITH
actor

CLARENCE THOMAS
Supreme Court justice

SOJOURNER TRUTH
antislavery activist

HARRIET TUBMAN
antislavery activist

NAT TURNER
slave revolt leader

DENMARK VESEY
slave revolt leader

ALICE WALKER
author

MADAM C. J. WALKER
entrepreneur

BOOKER T. WASHINGTON
educator

DENZEL WASHINGTON
actor

OPRAH WINFREY
entertainer

TIGER WOODS
golf star

RICHARD WRIGHT
author

1

A NIGHTMARE OR A DREAM?

— ❧ —

Situated on 125th Street between Seventh and Eighth Avenues in the heart of New York's Harlem district, the Apollo Theater stands as a testament to a rich African-American musical tradition. Built in the 1920s, the unassuming, gray, three-story building was originally an all-white music hall and burlesque theater. In January 1934, however, after the black cultural revolution known as the Harlem Renaissance had begun to wane, the Apollo came under new ownership. During its 60-year history as a black entertainment venue, the theater has featured a host of well-known African-American musicians, singers, and actors, including Josephine Baker, Lena Horne, Duke Ellington, Count Basie, Ella Fitzgerald, Jackie Wilson, James Brown, Aretha Franklin, and Richard Pryor.

But on May 6, 1995, the Apollo Theater was the setting for history of another kind. After 30 years of open and public hostility, two prominent black figures—Betty Shabazz, public relations director at Medgar Evers College in Brooklyn, New York, and widow of the slain activist Malcolm X, and Louis Farrakhan, the controversial leader of the Nation of Islam, met onstage in an emotional reunion. TV journalist Mike Wallace of CBS's news program 60 Minutes, who had covered the Nation of Islam since it began drawing national attention in the 1950s,

Harlem's historic Apollo Theater, site of the public reconciliation between Nation of Islam leader Louis Farrakhan and Betty Shabazz, the widow of Malcolm X.

called the event a "very meaningful and, indeed, historic moment."

Until that time, Betty Shabazz had repeatedly maintained that Farrakhan, a Nation of Islam minister in New York at the time of Malcolm X's assassination, had been responsible in part for her husband's death. During a television appearance only a few years earlier, she had been asked whether she believed that Farrakhan was directly involved. "Yes," she responded. "Nobody kept it a secret. It was a badge of honor. Everybody talked about it." In June 1994—less than a year before her appearance at the Apollo—she had appeared at a black leadership summit in Boston, Massachusetts, to which Farrakhan had also been invited. Although both were seated on

Qubilah Shabazz (center) is led from federal court after a preliminary hearing on charges stemming from her alleged attempt to hire a hit man to kill Louis Farrakhan.

the same stage, they did not speak to one another. Afterwards, her remarks to the press about the minister were decidedly cold; she reiterated her belief that he was involved in her husband's death and declared that she had not changed her position on the subject since the murder.

Their meeting at the Apollo, however, was the result of another tragic twist of fate affecting the personal lives of both leaders. In January of that year, Betty Shabazz's daughter Qubilah, who as a four-year-old had witnessed her father's death, was charged with conspiring to assassinate Louis Farrakhan.

A quiet, intelligent woman, Qubilah is the second-oldest of Malcolm and Betty Shabazz's four daughters and the least likely, family and childhood acquaintances said, to have reacted to her father's death by becoming involved in an assassination plot. But David Lillehaug, a U.S. attorney in Minneapolis, Minnesota, charged that Qubilah had spent seven months negotiating with a hit man to murder Farrakhan and had in fact moved to Minnesota to make a "down payment" on the crime. Lillehaug and the Federal Bureau of Investigation (FBI) claimed to have audio- and videotapes that proved her involvement. If convicted, Qubilah would have received a sentence of up to 90 years and would have been fined up to $2.5 million.

Although the conspiracy-murder charge itself was unexpected, Louis Farrakhan's response may not have been. Earlier that year, he had held a press conference specifically to address the charges against Qubilah Shabazz. Rather than holding the daughter of Malcolm X responsible for the plot, he accused the FBI of its own conspiracy to frame Qubilah in an attempt to discredit him, the Nation of Islam, and by extension, all African Americans. At the same time, he was filled with compassion for the daughter of his former mentor. "Qubilah is a child I knew and held in my arms as a baby," Farrakhan announced to a

Betty Shabazz wipes a tear from her eye during a news conference announcing the establishment of a defense fund for her daughter Qubilah, January 25, 1995.

crowd of 2,500 gathered in the Nation of Islam's Chicago temple. He continued:

> I do not believe that Qubilah is an evil woman. . . . Qubilah is a child who loves her father, who grieves over the loss of her father's life; a life cut short not by Louis Farrakhan but by the same evil forces who throw stones and hide their hands, and who . . . wash their hands and allow just men to go to an undeserved destruction.
>
> My wife is a righteous woman, my daughters are righteous women. They do not engage in unlawful acts. However, I assure you that if anyone were to do harm to me, they would not hesitate to avenge me. And they would not hire someone to do it for them, they would do it themselves! I believe that no power but Allah [God] could stop them.

If Qubilah were guilty of the charges against her, Farrakhan continued, she deserved forgiveness, not condemnation. The federal government had taken advantage of her grief and had "tricked" her into the appearance of an assassination plot.

The event at the Apollo Theater that May had been organized by Farrakhan himself in an effort to help pay for Qubilah's legal fees. The thousands of guests who witnessed the reconciliation had paid between $15 and $100 to attend. Only a few days before the event, the FBI had dropped the charges against Qubilah in exchange for two years of probation and counseling. Qubilah and her lawyers continued to maintain that she was the victim of entrapment by her friend Michael Fitzpatrick—an FBI informant—and the hit man that she had allegedly hired.

Under a banner that read in part, "All praise is due to Allah, Celebrating Unity," Betty Shabazz and Louis Farrakhan embraced warmly. Comparing the meeting to the first step in a long journey toward peace, Farrakhan prayed that Allah would bless their families with "total reconciliation." The government's plot against Qubilah, he continued, was "supposed to lure me into a fight with Betty Shabazz. Let us open the [government] files; they know that Farrakhan had nothing to do with the murder [of Malcolm X]."

"I never expected what I experienced here today," Betty Shabazz said in her speech. She thanked Farrakhan for his "original, gentle words of assurance" for her family and expressed gratitude "for the suggestion of support, as he said 'We will help brother Malcolm's family.' I like the way he said that. And I hope he continues to see my husband as brother Malcolm."

Until that day, a reconciliation between Betty Shabazz and Louis Farrakhan had been unimaginable to those who were familiar with their shared history. Was this the same man, many asked themselves, who 30 years earlier had declared Malcolm X "worthy of death" for "betraying" the Nation of Islam? Over the years, Farrakhan had repeatedly declared that he was innocent of any involvement in Malcolm's death.

Yet in a 1993 address about Malcolm X, he had thundered: "And if we [the Nation of Islam] dealt with him like a nation deals with a traitor, what the hell business is it of yours?"

Among whites and nonblack minorities, Louis Farrakhan is perhaps better known for such inflammatory rhetoric than for his willingness to forgive. In the last 10 years, the controversial leader of the Nation of Islam has increasingly come under fire for his anti-Semitic and antiwhite attacks, calling Jews "bloodsuckers" who run the world's businesses and governments, and whites "devils" who are responsible for the ills visited upon African Americans. Many feared that, during the most important appearance of his career, the 1995 Million Man March in Washington, D.C., Farrakhan's fiery words would incite rioting among the hundreds of thousands of black men gathered in the nation's capital.

But Farrakhan's message of independence and self-reliance has touched a nerve among African Americans. A recent poll of blacks showed that he is more familiar to them than every other prominent African American except politician Jesse Jackson and U.S. Supreme Court justice Clarence Thomas. Moreover, his powerful presence draws huge crowds: a 1992 lecture in Atlanta drew more attendees than a World Series game on the same night. He has drawn crowds of 25,000 or more in New York, and in Chicago, the headquarters of the Nation of Islam, he is known as the one black leader who can "fill a hall."

But Farrakhan also takes African Americans to task for self-neglect and immorality. During the Million Man March, he led the throng gathered before him in a pledge to avoid violence, to respect their families, and to improve their own communities through volunteer work and registering to vote.

Who is Louis Farrakhan? How did he rise to a position of power despite his hateful rhetoric? Clearly, his message of black autonomy fills a void for blacks who seek a strong, outspoken leader. Yet Farrakhan's popularity only makes his verbal attacks more potent. A man of remarkable contradictions, Farrakhan has characterized himself as a prophet, both of doom and of hope. "To some, I'm a nightmare," he has admitted, "but to others, I'm a dream come true."

2

"I JUST WANTED ANSWERS"

❧

The man who would become the leader of the Nation of Islam was born Louis Eugene Walcott on May 11, 1933. He was the second child of Sarah Mae Manning, a West Indies native who immigrated to the United States sometime during the mid-1920s. The circumstances surrounding Louis's birth were painful and complex.

Manning settled in the Bronx section of New York City and took work as a domestic for white employers. Soon after arriving, she met and married a cab driver named Percival Clarke, a Jamaican immigrant. But the marriage was not happy: Mae was unwilling to tolerate Clarke's infidelities, and Clarke began spending long periods of time away from home. During one of these absences, Mae met and fell in love with Louis Walcott, another cab driver. In October 1931, she had her first child, Alvan, by Walcott.

The following year, Clarke returned briefly, and Mae became pregnant again—this time by her husband. Fearful that Walcott would learn that she had been unfaithful to him, she tried three times to abort the pregnancy. Finally, in May 1933, she gave birth to her second child, Louis Eugene, whom she named after Walcott. Decades later, during a speech in Newark, New Jersey, Farrakhan would describe his mother's dilemma: "She's with a man, but I'm not his child. She don't want to tell the man, 'I've been

Louis Farrakhan as a young man.

unfaithful,' so she's hoping I'll be what he wanted: a girl. And she was hoping that I wouldn't be light . . . 'cause both my mother and the man she was living with were dark."

Farrakhan's comment led some observers to speculate that his biological father, Percival Clarke, was a white man. Some sources attest that Clarke's father was a white Portuguese man living in Jamaica. Though no one knows for sure, young Louis Eugene, or Gene, as his family and friends called him, suffered the alienation of being much lighter-skinned than his mother and brother.

When Gene was four years old, Mae Clarke and Louis Walcott moved with the boys to Boston, where they lived at 23 Melrose Street in the city's South End. Sometime between 1937 and 1938, Walcott and Clarke separated. Mae and her two children moved to 51 Westminster Street in the Roxbury neighborhood of the city, where they stayed for two years. In 1940, they moved once again, finally settling on Shawmut Avenue in Roxbury.

Shawmut Avenue was situated in the heart of a close-knit community of West Indian immigrants who valued education and discipline above all. Like many northeastern cities during the 1940s, Boston was filled with people from many nations and backgrounds. In the three previous decades, nearly three million African Americans had left the South to seek their fortunes in the more industrialized North. And during World War I, millions of Europeans flooded into America seeking political and economic freedom. A great percentage of these immigrants settled in the Northeast. When returning war veterans joined the workforce beginning in 1917, white workers feared losing their jobs to blacks and race relations in America deteriorated. The fierce competition for jobs and housing also led to discord among different groups of immigrants and between newcomers and longtime residents of northeastern cities.

For Mae Clarke and her sons, Roxbury offered some measure of unity and security, but ethnic and racial tensions were always present. In his book *Boston Boy*, journalist Nat Hentoff relates how he, like other Jewish children in Boston, was ridiculed and beaten by black children. Likewise, Hentoff notes, at the Dudley Street trolley station in Roxbury, blacks would often jump from trolley cars and run to avoid being harassed by Irish or Italian residents. Gene Walcott was sometimes among those targeted for attack.

Boston's Roxbury neighborhood near Highland Park, circa 1947. Farrakhan, born Louis Eugene Walcott, grew up in this section of Boston, where he lived with his mother, Mae, and older brother, Alvan.

Such distrust and mistreatment also occurred between members of the same race. For instance, blacks already living in the area resented newly arrived West Indian immigrants. They called them "Jewmaicans" because they preferred to worship in the Anglican St. Cyprian's Church rather than in American black churches and because they were believed to be wealthier and thus in a class with local Jewish families, for whom many black women worked as domestics. Biographers and commentators have speculated that the intraracial hatred Farrakhan experienced—being called a Jew by fellow blacks who disapproved of and disliked Jews—may have played a part in forming his virulent anti-Semitism.

Civility was very important in the West Indian community of Roxbury, and Mae Clarke instructed her children to avoid fighting at all costs. But one day when he was 13, Gene ignored his mother's rule. "I punched a white boy in front of my friends," Farrakhan recalled. "I was trying to show off. He didn't do anything to me. It bothered my conscience. That boy did nothing to me, although, of course, he was a member of a group that did much to me and my people. I felt bad. . . . That's the only incident where I struck somebody."

As she had in New York, Clarke struggled to support her children. When she could not find work, she was forced to go on welfare. At other times, she earned money cleaning, pressing, and repairing clothing or working as a housekeeper for white employers, many of whom were physicians at Massachusetts General Hospital. Among her employers were a number of Jewish families. One man for whom she worked in the 1950s remembers Clarke's strict enforcement of table manners and her extensive knowledge of the Jewish dietary code. "She just stepped in and knew immediately what to do," he said. "My wife had recently died, and I had three small children. She was great with them."

Alvan and Gene attended the Asa Gray Elementary School and the Sherwin School, both within blocks of their home. Like other Caribbean immigrants, Mae Clarke firmly believed that a proper education included musical training. Although money was scarce, she managed to save enough to pay for piano lessons for seven-year-old Alvan and violin lessons for six-year-old Gene. After a few years studying under a local teacher, Gene began taking lessons from a Russian Jewish immigrant. By the time he was in high school, playing the violin had become his passion. He would practice for up to five hours each day. "I liked to play in the bathroom," Farrakhan remembered. "The violin seemed to resonate better there, and I could watch myself better in the mirror. Nobody could get into the bathroom while I was playing."

A bright and diligent student, Gene was also an active member of St. Cyprian's Episcopal Church, which had been established by the black Caribbeans of Boston. In addition to serving as an acolyte (a minister's assistant) and singing in the choir, he regularly played his violin at Sunday concerts. But the young churchgoer could not understand "why it was an honor to go downtown to sing with a white choir in a white church," as St. Cyprian's choir occasionally did. He would wonder "why, if God had sent a deliverer to an oppressed people in the past, why that same God wouldn't send us a deliverer? I never heard my pastor speak on the question of the liberation of my people. . . . I loved Jesus and I loved scripture, but I just wanted answers."

Next door to St. Cyprian's was Toussaint L'Ouverture Hall, home of the local branch of the Universal Negro Improvement Association (UNIA), an organization intent on promoting black pride. A Jamaican man named Marcus Garvey had formed the UNIA in 1914 after witnessing the brutal treatment of his fellow West Indian workers. The movement failed to take hold in Garvey's native country, however, and in 1916 he shifted its headquarters to Harlem, New York, one of the largest African-American communities in the country and a thriving black business and cultural center. By 1919, the UNIA claimed a worldwide membership of two million, with branches in Chicago, Philadelphia, New Orleans, and Los Angeles. The organization eventually became the largest black social movement in American history.

At the heart of Garvey's movement was his desire to see blacks educate themselves so that they

"I cried and cried because Marcus Garvey was dead," Farrakhan would recollect of the day when, as an 11-year-old, he both found out who Marcus Garvey was and learned that Garvey had died. Garvey (right) had founded the Universal Negro Improvement Association.

could achieve economic independence and political power. He urged them to take pride in their race and to free themselves from dependence on white employers and institutions. "Where is the black man's Government?" Garvey would ask. "Where is his King, his kingdom, his navy, his men of big affairs?" He had never seen such things, he would tell his listeners, and he would then declare, "I will help to make them."

Traveling widely through the United States and Canada, the dynamic Garvey spoke tirelessly about the need for universal solidarity among blacks and about the importance of working to raise oneself out of poverty and oppression. "Up, you mighty race!" he would cry. "You can accomplish what you will!" His words thrilled African Americans who had grown restless and discouraged by racial injustice and economic hardship, and UNIA membership continued to increase.

In 1918, Garvey, a former printer, began publishing *Negro World*, a weekly newspaper for the UNIA. Filled with information on events and issues of interest to blacks, the paper was distributed in the United States, Canada, the West Indies, Latin America, Europe, and Africa, with a peak circulation of more than 60,000. Through *Negro World*, many readers gained their first glimpse of black life in other parts of the world.

Unlike the country's more moderate black leaders of the time—such as W. E. B. Du Bois, the head of the National Association for the Advancement of Colored People (NAACP)—Garvey strongly opposed integration efforts, favoring black separatism instead. In fact, as time went by, Garvey promoted himself as a black Moses struggling to lead his people back to their African homeland. Though this dream was never realized, black separatist groups kept alive his Back-to-Africa concept for many decades.

Headquartered on Tremont Street in Roxbury,

Ted Mack, host of The Ted Mack Original Amateur Hour, *a nationally televised talent show. As a 16-year-old, Gene Walcott, an accomplished violinist, played classical music on Mack's show.*

the Boston branch of the UNIA thrived, particularly among the neighborhood's Caribbean immigrants. Although Mae Clarke was not a member of the UNIA, she was most likely sympathetic to its tenets, and the organization's strong presence allowed Gene to be introduced to it at an early age. One member of his family appears to have been an ardent Garveyite: in 1944, while visiting his uncle in New York, 11-year-old Gene noticed a picture of a black man on the mantlepiece and asked who he was. "The greatest leader our people [have] ever had," replied his uncle, explaining the teachings of Garvey. Gene excitedly asked where Garvey could be found. "He's dead," his uncle said. Farrakhan later described his sorrow over the news: "[I] was so hurt that after hoping, all my young years, to meet the right man for our people, that when I found him, he was already dead. . . . I cried and cried because Marcus Garvey was dead."

When Gene was 14, his grades were high enough that he was offered a place in the city's elite Boston Latin School. The oldest public school in America, Boston Latin is the alma mater of such notable Americans as Benjamin Franklin, patriot Samuel Adams, theologian Cotton Mather, author Ralph Waldo Emerson, and composer Leonard Bernstein. But Gene felt unhappy and out of place with the extremely rigorous academic schedule and the nearly all-white student body, and after one year he transferred to English High, another school with an excellent academic reputation. There, as a member of a student body that was 15 percent black, Gene flourished. He joined the track team and became a minor celebrity. "In those days, being a track star was like being a president," one of his neighbors remembered. "Louis was 'the president' of Roxbury. But he wouldn't flaunt it. . . . It wasn't important to him. He would go home and do his homework and wouldn't bathe in the glory just because he had won a fifty-yard dash."

In addition to his athletic endeavors, Gene remained devoted to music throughout his teens. When he was 16, a New York calypso group called Joe Clark and His Calypsonians came to Roxbury for a fund-raising concert. Gene was struck by the new sound. "I can do that," he said to John Bynoe, a friend who had organized the event. That same year, while continuing to attend school, Gene began performing in the city's black nightclubs as "The Charmer."

Not surprisingly, Gene's prim mother was dismayed and confused by her son's decision to perform such spirited music in public places. "She came a few times when I was in the nightclub . . . singing the

Although his hometown of Boston had its share of racial and ethnic tensions, it was not until Farrakhan traveled to North Carolina to attend Winston-Salem Teachers' College that he first encountered official segregation.

music of the Caribbean," Farrakhan recalled, and "she would register some of her disapproval of my gyrations in my dance and some of the songs that I sung." But in Massachusetts Avenue clubs like Eddie's Lounge and the Hi-Hat, Gene began drawing attention. On May 15, 1949, he appeared on national television on *The Ted Mack Original Amateur Hour,* performing classical music on his violin. In contrast to the crooning, swaying image he portrayed in his nightclub act, Gene's debut on television showed him as a clean-cut, polite, and promising young man, conservatively dressed in a suit and tie. "You're just a champion at heart, aren't you?" Ted Mack remarked, after questioning the young performer about his ambitions.

—Like many high school students, Gene Walcott began thinking about college during his senior year. Still serious about pursuing a musical career, he considered attending the Juilliard School of Music in New York, but he never applied because he knew that his family would not be able to afford the tuition. Eventually, he decided on Winston-Salem Teachers' College, an all-black school in North Carolina, in part because he received a track scholarship to the school, but also because he felt a need to understand the injustices and hardships that black southerners experienced. He began his first semester there in September 1950.

Walcott had not even arrived in the South before he encountered for the first time the horrors of official segregation and overt racism. During a lengthy stopover between trains in Washington, D.C., he decided to see a movie. As he walked toward the theater, he received stares and odd looks from patrons and theater employees. Finally, one of them turned him away. "We don't sell tickets to niggers," the cashier told him. When he arrived in North Carolina, he discovered separate water fountains and bathroom facilities for whites and blacks, something he had never seen in the North despite the racial and ethnic tension of immigrant Boston. On the few occasions when he dared to drink from a "white fountain," Gene met with glares from strangers and embarrassed glances from classmates. And though the city of Winston-Salem did not segregate its public transportation, it did have its own bus company for blacks—fittingly called the Safe Bus Company.

As in high school, Gene joined the Winston-Salem track team, running the 440- and 880-yard relays and the 100- and 200-yard dashes. And he soon learned that discrimination didn't stop at the college's doors. Winston-Salem had to share the local track with another, all-white, school: Wake Forest University, whose team always had the track first. Winston-Salem's athletes were warned not to "cause trouble" by socializing with Wake Forest students.

Walcott was not a perfect student; he often had to

The success of calypso singer Harry Belafonte (above) inspired Farrakhan to try his luck as a performer. After dropping out of college, he launched a musical career as "Calypso Gene."

be coaxed out of bed by his roommates to make his early morning classes. Instead, he remained devoted to music. When he was not on the track, he practiced his violin for hours. Walcott still loved the calypso music he had first heard as a teenager; he even organized his own band, which performed statewide. As a freshman at Winston-Salem, he was featured in the school's yearly talent night as The Charmer, the persona he had adopted in his Boston nightclub appearances. Among his original songs was one he called "Why America Is No Democracy." The sentiments he expressed in this piece would echo years later in his first recorded song, "A White Man's Heaven Is a Black Man's Hell," which he would write as a newly converted minister for the Nation of Islam.

⌐Although the female students at Winston-Salem outnumbered the male students by a great margin, the athlete and musician displayed little interest in dating women he met in college. That became even more true, recalls one of his classmates, when Walcott met and fell in love with a young Roxbury woman named Betsy Ross while at home on a semester break in 1950. After that, his friend said, "He never made time for anyone else and he never looked at anyone else."

 ⌐ Gene had lost much of his enthusiasm for college by the time he returned to Winston-Salem to begin his sophomore year. He felt homesick for Roxbury and he missed Betsy. But something else was on his mind. That year, he had heard about a young African-American calypso singer named Harry Belafonte whose music was quickly becoming popular across the country. Frustrated with his own progress as a performer, he decided during the summer of 1953 to drop out of college and pursue a music career. Mae Clarke was furious and insisted that her son stay in school.

But he did not return to college, and on September 12, 1953, 20-year-old Gene Walcott and 17-year-old Betsy Ross were married in St. Cyprian's Church. Only two years later, Gene's life would change forever.

3

THE ORIGINAL MEN

❦

Gene and Betsy's first child, a daughter, was born the year after they were married, and with no college degree and a family to support, Walcott resumed his stage career. By this time "Calypso Gene," as he had begun billing himself, had earned a considerable reputation, both in the Midwest and in New England, where his fans claimed him as a local talent.

Walcott not only performed, he also acted as his own agent and publicity manager. An employee for the black newspaper *Boston Graphic* remembers receiving publicity shots of Walcott posed in tropical shirts from the performer himself. Once again appearing in Massachusetts Avenue clubs—and even closer to his former home, at Butler Hall on Tremont Street—Calypso Gene thrilled local club audiences and amazed those who remembered him as a studious, violin-playing young man.

Gene worked hard to earn money to support his family, but he was known to give impromptu—and free—concerts in his old neighborhood. John Rice, a Roxbury resident who had grown up near the Walcotts and considered Gene a "big brother," recounts one memorable day:

> [I was] playing softball in Madison Park when we saw a band coming down Ruggles Street on the back of a flat-bed truck. The music sounded so Cuban, so rhythmic. People started dropping their balls and bats and

Nation of Islam leader Elijah Muhammad (center, holding book). After Farrakhan heard "the Messenger" speak at a Savior's Day rally in February 1955, he joined the Black Muslims.

gloves, and other people started dancing all down the street and then down another street. And then I saw that it was Eugene Walcott. He was a show.

Despite Calypso Gene's rising popularity, he would never attain national stardom as a musician and singer. Although he was approached by at least one record company, Walcott was frustrated and angered by the attempts of white record executives to tell him how to run his own show. One account notes that his "attitude problems" prevented him from being signed. In any case, he would be completely unprepared for the dramatic event that would change his life in February 1955.

The Walcotts were in Chicago, Illinois, that month in the midst of an eight-week tour called the "Calypso Follies," in which Gene headlined, when Gene ran into an old friend, Rodney Smith. Smith mentioned that he had recently converted to a religion called the Nation of Islam. In fact, he said, the Nation was holding its annual convention— called Savior's Day—that month in its main temple, at 5335 South Greenwood Avenue in the city's South Side. He persuaded the Walcotts to attend.

On February 26, Gene and Betsy, accompanied by Gene's uncle, arrived at the temple and seated themselves in the balcony. Listening to Elijah Muhammad, the Nation of Islam's leader, Farrakhan recalls, he was impressed by Muhammad's ideas but did not think much of the man's uneducated way of speaking. All at once, Muhammad looked up toward Walcott and said, "Brother, don't pay attention to how I speak. Pay attention to what I'm saying. I didn't get the chance to go to the white man's fine schools, because when I tried to go, the doors were closed. But if you take what I say and place it into the beautiful way of speaking you know, you can help me save our people."

Walcott was stunned. He would later learn that Muhammad was informed of the "college man" in

the audience "who could help us if we get him" and that Muhammad knew where he would be sitting. But at that moment, Gene was convinced that the Messenger, as Elijah Muhammad was called, could read his mind. That day, Eugene Walcott joined the Nation of Islam.

A relatively new movement among African Americans, the Nation of Islam had been founded less than 30 years before Gene Walcott's first encounter with it. Originally called the Lost-Found Nation of Islam, it developed from a movement more religiously oriented but similar to Marcus Garvey's UNIA—the Moorish Temple of America. Founded in 1915 by a North Carolina man named Noble Drew Ali after he had visited Morocco, the Moorish Temple maintained that African Americans should adopt Islam and refer to themselves as Moorish

Blacks and whites stand in a relief line at the height of the Great Depression. Though no group was spared the ravages of the depression, African Americans were particularly hard hit. From these desperate times emerged the Lost-Found Nation of Islam.

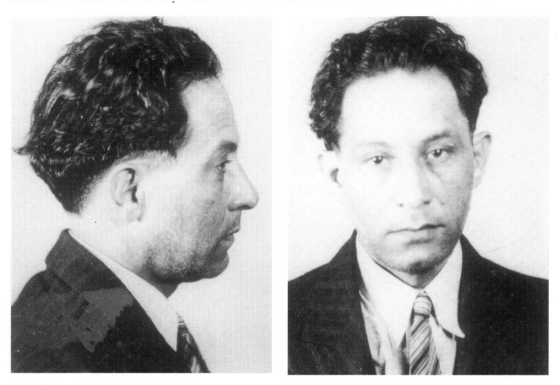

The mysterious Wallace Fard, self-proclaimed prophet from Arabia and founder of the Lost-Found Nation of Islam, taught that blacks were the chosen people and whites the embodiment of evil.

Americans (the Moors having originally lived in present-day Morocco and Algeria). "When each group has its own peculiar religion," Ali taught his followers, "there will be peace on earth."

Ali's teachings spread to blacks in the Midwest, and eventually he issued identification cards to his followers that bore the symbols of Islam: a star and crescent, an image of clasped hands, and an encircled number seven. The cards also declared that the bearer believed in "all the Divine Prophets, Jesus, Muhammad, Buddha, and Confucius."

Ali's version of Islam was not orthodox; rather, it came from a variety of sources, including Eastern philosophy, the Quran, and the Bible. He also drew on assorted anecdotes about Jesus Christ and Marcus Garvey. Moorish Temple members were required to adhere to strict rules of conduct: they were forbidden to attend movie theaters or dance halls and were not to use cosmetics, tobacco, alcohol, or other products believed to be unclean or unhealthful. Ali's teachings emphasized a healthy diet and natural herbal remedies, and they were often paired with the sale of charms, relics, and magical potions.

To make themselves appear more like their African counterparts, Ali's male followers donned red fezzes and grew beards. Accompanying this new look was an open contempt for police and for whites, whom the Moorish Americans called Europeans.

By the mid-1920s, the Moorish Temple of America had attracted droves of newcomers, many of whom were former Garveyites. But in 1929, Noble Drew Ali was implicated in a murder, and his movement fell apart. He died soon after from what were said to be mysterious causes.

At about the same time, the crash of the New York Stock Exchange ravaged the entire nation, marking the beginning of an economic depression that lasted into World War II. Millions of Americans lost their jobs and their homes. African Americans were among those who suffered most severely. Black workers were usually the first to be let go; nearly half of those who lost their jobs had been domestic servants and were replaced by white workers. Black unemployment soared to 50 percent nationwide and reached as high as 80 percent in some cities.

Although the UNIA and the Moorish Temple of America had died out by this time, African Americans increasingly sought solace in black-founded religious and political organizations. The Lost-Found Nation of Islam was among the more radical movements to form during this period.

The founder of the Nation of Islam was Wallace Fard, a small, earnest, light-skinned man of unknown origin who arrived in Detroit, Michigan, during the summer of 1930. Acting as a door-to-door peddler, Fard told blacks that he was a prophet from Arabia who had come to the United States to help them discover their dual African and Islamic heritages.

The Nation of Islam drew on various sources. This page: The Bible. Opposite page: Joseph F. "Judge" Rutherford, leader of the Jehovah's Witnesses.

Blacks were the chosen people, Fard said. In fact, the first humans to walk the earth had been black, "long before the white man stood up on his hind legs and crept out of the caves of Europe."

The white man, Fard asserted, was the devil himself, the embodiment of evil. He had enslaved blacks and robbed them of their African names, replacing them with Christian names. To reclaim their rightful place in the world, every black should adopt an Islamic name or use an X or combination of X's and other letters to symbolize his or her spiritual rebirth. If they joined the Nation of Islam, Fard told his listeners, they would learn once again to respect their heritage, develop a sense of discipline, and work to overcome their white oppressors.

In an atmosphere of resignation and despair, Fard offered hope to African Americans. Within three years of his arrival in Detroit, he had recruited and organized 8,000 followers. By 1934, the Nation of Islam had become a cohesive community that included an elementary school for Muslim children, training classes for women on how to be proper wives and mothers, and a private security force.

Among Fard's most zealous followers was a young man named Elijah Poole, a native of the small coastal town of Sandersville, Georgia (the Poole surname had been taken from the white slaveholding family who owned Elijah's grandparents). Like thousands of African Americans, Poole and his family had traveled north during the Great Migration and had settled in Detroit, in 1923. During the 1920s, the Poole house—which lacked many bare essentials, including a toilet—would hold four children. Clara, Elijah Poole's wife, worked as a domestic to help support the family.

With the stock market crash, Poole lost his job and took his place with millions of others in relief lines. The family subsisted mainly on such meals as boiled chicken feet and discarded vegetables salvaged from grocery store garbage cans. Coal to heat the house was collected from the beds along railroad tracks, and Clara clothed the children in worn garments given to her by the people for whom she cleaned, washed, and ironed.

For two years, Poole remained on relief. He left the house before dawn every morning to stand in lines with thousands of unemployed people seeking work in local manufacturing plants. At times, he would wait in line all morning.

Considering Elijah Poole's desperate economic struggles—and a background that included both a deeply religious upbringing and a familiarity with Islam—it is perhaps not surprising that he became one of Wallace Fard's most enthusiastic followers. While growing up in Georgia, he had lived among many blacks whose ancestors were African Muslims. They continued to practice their faith even after they were enslaved and brought to America, and they passed down their Islamic practices and beliefs to their descendants. Others may have adopted Islam as a means of rejecting Christianity, which had been forced upon their ancestors by white slave owners.

Elijah's parents were not Muslims. His father, Wali, was a Baptist minister, and Elijah and his 12 brothers and sisters grew up listening to their father's fiery sermons. Early on, however, Elijah began to feel that Christianity would not release African Americans from oppression, as many of them seemed to expect. Although he felt a religious calling, he later told his mother, he could not "preach the Christian religion. . . . something [was] warning me that this is not right."

Poole was still searching for a spiritual home when he moved north with his family. Seven years later, in 1930, he found it. His father had urged him to hear the preaching of Abdul Muhammad, who had been a member of the Moorish Temple of America and had converted to the Nation of Islam. Elijah was intrigued by the man's message, and after hearing Wallace Fard himself speak, he was convinced that he had discovered his true ministry.

Poole's first encounter with Fard in the fall of 1931 marked a turning point in the development of the Nation of Islam. Poole later said of Fard,

> I recognized him to be God in person, and that is what he said he was, but he forbade me to tell anyone else. I was a student of the Bible. I recognized him to be the person the Bible predicted would come two thousand years after Jesus' death. It came to me the first time I laid eyes on him.

Poole was given an Islamic name, Elijah Muhammad, and soon became Fard's chief lieutenant, helping him to rouse support and recruit new members for the movement. Fard quickly adopted the role Poole ascribed to him, presenting himself as Allah, or "the Jesus" for whom his followers had been waiting.

The Nation of Islam attracted controversy from the start, especially over its doctrine that whites are inherently evil. Fard drew his movement's principles from the Quran, the Bible, Freemasonry books, and the philosophy of Joseph F. "Judge" Rutherford, the leader of the Jehovah's Witnesses (a religious movement that focuses on the second coming of Christ). But its tale of creation is unique.

According to Fard, the world was initially ruled by a highly advanced civilization of blacks, the original inhabitants of an enormous planet several times larger than earth, who lived in the city of Mecca. Their scientists were powerful men who formed the mountains and the seas and populated the land with various animals. When an explosion divided the planet into the earth and the moon, the survivors, called the "original men," settled in the fertile Nile Valley and became known as the Tribe of Shabazz. They lived peacefully for 6,000 years, until evil entered the world in the form of a mad scientist named Yacub.

Yacub wanted absolute power over his people,

The flag of the Nation of Islam.

and he set out to attain it by applying the principles of magnetism—that unlike forces attract each other and like forces repel—to people. He created a race of light-skinned "unlike men" and drew followers by teaching his ideas to others. In doing so, he broke the laws of Islam, and he and his followers were exiled from Mecca to the island of Pelan (believed to be near present-day Greece).

Enraged, Yacub was determined to exact vengeance. Using his knowledge of genetics, he created from his followers over the next 600 years a race of immoral men, "white devils," who returned to Mecca to avenge themselves, causing disruption and endless trouble for the original black inhabitants. Finally, the whites were rounded up and banished to Europe.

In Europe, they gradually gained dominion over the world. They committed countless atrocities, including taking blacks into slavery, stripping them of their language and their culture, and brainwashing them into believing that whites were their superiors. It was time, said Fard, for the 6,000-year rule of the "blue-eyed devils" to end. To bring that about, blacks needed to become aware of their shared history and their destiny as rulers of the world. Fard told his followers that he, the *Mahdi,* or almighty being, would lead them back to their original state of grace.

Although the Nation of Islam's religious doctrines may sound extreme and his proclamation of divinity sacrilegious, his supporters believed in him and in his larger message of racial pride. To the Black Muslims, as Nation of Islam members came to be called, Fard's version of the history of mankind was no less believable than the biblical story of creation.

But Fard gave his followers more than hope: he offered the means to help them improve their lives. As Noble Drew Ali's adherents had done, Black Muslims followed a strict set of dietary and behavioral guidelines. They were forbidden to eat foods like cornbread, black-eyed peas, chitlins, and pork, which were considered unhealthful and part of a "slave diet." They were not to engage in behavior such as gambling, smoking tobacco, drinking alcohol, or taking drugs, and they were required at all times to dress neatly and to be well spoken and respectful of others. Moreover, after Elijah Muhammad rose in rank and eventually assumed leadership of the Nation of Islam, he determined that the movement would help improve the lives of black Americans not only spiritually but also socially and economically, by establishing programs for the poor and the unemployed.

By the time Gene and Betsy Walcott heard the words of Elijah Muhammad at the Nation's annual convention in February 1955, Muhammad had been the movement's leader for 21 years. Betsy was so moved by his speech that she signed up immediately when new members were recruited at the end of the meeting. Despite Muhammad's overwhelming effect on him, Gene had to be coaxed to join that day by his uncle. Months later, however, after hearing the ardent words of the Nation's greatest minister, Malcolm X, Gene finally became certain that the Nation of Islam was the path he was destined to follow. He recalls:

> [As a Christian] I hated the fact that . . . we talked about the 'love of Christ,' but I didn't feel the love of white Christians toward black Christians. And that the church was unwilling—or unable—to address specific concerns of black people for justice. I went looking not for a new religion, but for new leadership that would address the concerns of black people. And I found Malcolm X and Elijah Muhammad. I was not interested in changing my religion, but they were Muslims and they spoke a truth that I could identify with.

The 11-year-old boy who had wept at the death of Marcus Garvey had at last found a means to save his people.

4

PROPHETS IN THEIR OWN LAND

❦

As with the UNIA and the Moorish Temple of America, the Nation of Islam's reclusiveness and unorthodox beliefs almost immediately attracted the attention of law enforcement authorities. In Detroit, rumors arose that the Nation was a cult practicing human sacrifice, and Fard was arrested three times for allegedly encouraging such practices. In the spring of 1933, authorities ordered Fard to leave town. He traveled to Chicago, where Elijah Muhammad had established the Nation's Temple Number Two, but he was immediately arrested again and jailed by local authorities. In his absence, Fard appointed Muhammad chief official, responsible for the Nation's administrative affairs and minister of Temple Number One in Detroit.

No sooner had Muhammad assumed leadership than trouble arose between the Detroit police and the Nation. The city government alleged that Black Muslims were attempting to persuade black schoolchildren to study at the Nation's University of Islam. Alerted by the Michigan State Board of Education that the Nation of Islam's school was not accredited, authorities arrested teachers at the university.

Muhammad was also arrested and charged with contributing to the delinquency of minors. Upon hearing of his arrest, 700 unarmed Black Muslims marched to police headquarters in protest. They

Spreading the word during the Nation of Islam's 1964 Savior's Day convention in Chicago.

43

were met by billy-club-wielding police and forced to disperse. Authorities ultimately offered to drop all charges provided the Nation of Islam enroll its children in public schools within six months. Muhammad refused and moved the Nation's headquarters to Chicago.

Shortly after this episode, around June 1934, Fard disappeared—as mysteriously, it seems, as he had arrived. Many of his followers believed that he had returned to Mecca (the holiest city of Islam) to prepare for the end of the world. Other Nation of Islam members claimed that the police had killed him, and Muhammad himself declared that Fard had been deported. But critics of the Black Muslim movement speculated that Fard's disappearance and Muhammad's subsequent rise to power were more than coincidental.

The disappearance of the organization's founder sparked internal conflicts that threatened the Nation's very existence. When Muhammad, at odds with other factions, established a separate branch of the Nation called the Temple People, his rivals were so angered that Muhammad fled Chicago in fear for his life. He left his wife, Clara, and five children behind, where he believed they would remain safe.

For the next seven years Muhammad traveled across the United States under assumed names and continued preaching the doctrine of the Temple of Islam. Thus, although the organization's earliest tenets originated with Wallace Fard, Elijah Muhammad was most responsible for developing and spreading the precepts and practices that shaped today's Nation of Islam.

In Chicago, Muhammad's wife directed the Temple's development in her husband's absence. The new group, greatly reduced in size, gathered regularly in private homes. When Muhammad returned to Chicago in 1941, the Temple of Islam once again began to prosper and soon surpassed the size of the

original Nation of Islam. The Temple adopted the name of the now-defunct Nation, and its members began renting halls in Chicago's South Side ghetto. These meeting places became known as Temples of Islam.

In December 1941, soon after Muhammad returned to Chicago, the United States entered World War II. Maintaining that Black Muslims were forbidden to bear arms or perform acts of violence unless directed by Allah, he and his followers refused to register for the military draft. Five months later, Muhammad and 11 other black leaders were arrested and imprisoned for draft avoidance and sedition (encouraging others to break the law). Muhammad himself received a sentence of five years.

Handcuffed to a U.S. marshal, Elijah Muhammad walks to court. When the United States entered World War II in December 1941, Muhammad urged his followers to refuse to register for the draft. He was sentenced to five years in prison for draft avoidance and sedition.

While he and the others served their sentences, the burden of keeping the Nation going once again fell on the shoulders of Black Muslim women, who collected iron, paper, and other items and sold them to keep the Nation afloat financially. Muhammad's wife, now known as Sister Clara, was especially active in running Chicago's Temple Number Two. And because she maintained close contact with her husband, Muhammad was able to retain control of his organization.

After his release from prison in 1946, Elijah Muhammad returned to Chicago to resume his position as leader of the Nation of Islam. The years that he had spent in flight and in prison did not diminish his stature among the Nation's followers. Instead, his "exile" was viewed as proof of his dedication. Muham-

A group of Black Muslim women attend a hearing in the sedition case against Elijah Muhammad and other Nation of Islam leaders. During the war years—while its leaders were in prison—the Nation was held together by women.

mad took advantage of such admiration by comparing himself to the persecuted prophets of the Bible and the Quran. Like Mohammed, the founder of the Islamic religion and the last prophet of Allah, Elijah Muhammad became known as the Last Messenger of Wallace Fard, sent to inform African Americans of their original status as rulers of the earth.

In 1941, around the same time that Elijah Muhammad was arrested and jailed for draft avoidance, an angry teenager named Malcolm Little arrived in Gene Walcott's Roxbury neighborhood. Although they lived in the same area of Boston, the two came from vastly different backgrounds. They would not meet until years later—under greatly changed circumstances.

Malcolm's father, Earl, was an ardent follower of Marcus Garvey, and young Malcolm often attended UNIA meetings with him. But unlike Gene Walcott, Malcolm had grown up in an atmosphere steeped in racial violence. Shortly before his birth in 1925, his family was driven out of Omaha, Nebraska, by the Ku Klux Klan. They settled in Lansing, Michigan, where Earl felt that he could establish his own black-rights organization. In 1929, when Malcolm was four years old, another white hate group known as the White Legionnaires set fire to the Littles' house. Earl ran outside with a pistol, firing at the arsonists and shouting warnings to his family. They barely escaped. Years later, Malcolm would describe the horror of the incident: "I remember being snatched awake into a frightening confusion of pistol shots and shouting and smoke and flames," he recalled. "Our home was burning down around us. . . . The white police and firemen came and stood around watching as the house burned to the ground."

A fearless activist, Earl Little was often the target of harassment and threats by white supremacists. One day in 1931, only a few hours after he had left home, his body was found along the downtown trolley

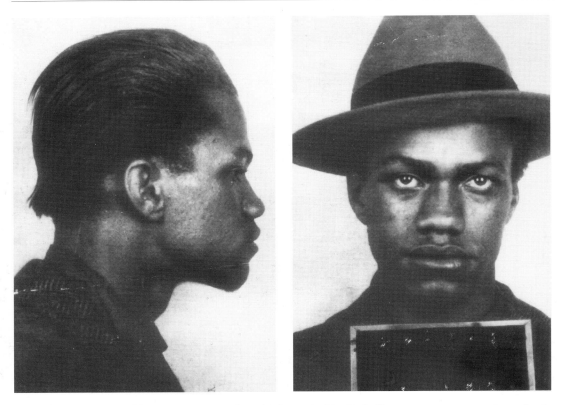

Mug shots of 18-year-old Malcolm Little, arrested in Boston in 1944 for larceny. While serving time in prison for a 1945 robbery, Little became acquainted with the teachings of Elijah Muhammad and changed his name to Malcolm X.

tracks. Although Earl's killers were never identified, his friends and family, including Malcolm, were certain that he was a victim of white supremacists.

Louise Little, left alone to provide for eight children during the height of the Great Depression, was forced to accept public relief. Despite the family's determination to remain together, welfare investigators frequently visited the Little household in an attempt to break it up. Finally, in 1937, Louise broke down under the intense pressure and was committed to a mental institution, and her children were made wards of the state. The youngest of them, including 12-year-old Malcolm, were separated from one another and placed in foster homes.

Angry and alienated, Malcolm had already clashed with the law on several occasions by this time. At age 13, he was sent to a juvenile detention center, despite his great academic promise. Finally, when he was 15 years old, his half-sister, Ella, a child from Earl Little's first marriage, offered to have Malcolm live with her in Boston.

Malcolm tried hard to rebuild his life, becoming a shoe shiner and then a soda-fountain clerk to earn money for himself. But the teenager was intoxicated by the excitement and danger of living in a big city, and he eventually began selling and using drugs. Soon after, he gave up his job because it prevented him from enjoying the nightlife of Boston.

In 1941—the year that Elijah Muhammad was arrested for draft avoidance—Malcolm Little moved to New York and settled in a boardinghouse in Harlem, one of the leading centers of African-American culture. Before long, he became embroiled in the New York underworld of thievery, drug dealing, and prostitution. Ella and his Boston acquaintances were alarmed at Malcom's transformation when he returned to that city. In 1945, at age 20, Malcolm was arrested and sentenced to jail for robbery.

Rebellious and hostile, Malcolm relished the nickname of "Satan" that he earned from his fellow inmates at Boston's Charlestown State Prison. He was frequently placed in solitary confinement for his behavior, but he enjoyed being alone and would pace his cell, railing against everything and everyone in savage, antireligious outbursts.

Malcolm delivered one such verbal attack on an older prisoner named Bimbi while working in the prison workshop. Without raising his voice or using profanity, Bimbi demolished Malcolm's argument. It was the younger man's first encounter with someone who was able to "command total respect . . . with his words."

Intrigued by Bimbi's unusual power, Malcolm began studying in the prison library and enrolled in correspondence courses. Before long, he began seeing himself not as a lone black youth whose experiences no one else could fathom, but as a member of a larger group struggling to find its place in American society. By 1948, when Malcolm was transferred to Norfolk Prison in Massachusetts, his brothers Philbert and Reginald and his sister Hilda had begun writing to him about the Nation of Islam. Malcolm was ready to listen.

Malcolm was deeply moved by the teachings of Elijah Muhammad. "[T]he white devil has hidden it from you, that you are a race of people of ancient civilizations," Reginald wrote. "You have been cut off by the devil white man from all true knowledge of your own kind." In Malcolm's experience, this was true. Much of the hardship and pain in his life could be attributed to whites, and he had read widely about the horrors of slavery in the Americas and about European colonialism in Africa. He eagerly embraced Elijah Muhammad's teachings and embarked on a demanding regimen of self-improvement.

Malcolm began spending hours in the prison library, devouring books on philosophy, history, science, religion, and spirituality. He became courteous and respectful, to the amazement of fellow inmates and guards. To symbolize his new affiliation with the Nation of Islam, he abandoned his "slave name" of Little and replaced it with the letter X.

Having been awarded an early release from prison for good behavior, Malcolm traveled to Detroit to live with his brother Wilfred. He was overwhelmed with reverence at his first meeting with Elijah Muhammad. Inspired by the Messenger's exhortation to attract new members, Malcolm X became an enthusiastic and effective recruiter for the Nation, and he embarked on "fishing" expeditions to bars, poolrooms, and street corners in poor sections of Detroit. Having been an outcast and criminal himself, he understood the experiences of others in those situations, and he was able to persuade many of them to reform. In the same way, he attracted a great number of prison inmates to the Nation of Islam.

In 1953, only a year after his release from prison, Malcolm X was named assistant minister of Temple Number One. A gifted and charismatic speaker, he began traveling across the country to organize new temples and visit those already established.

Due in great part to the zealous efforts of Malcolm X, the Nation of Islam expanded at a tremendous rate in the 1950s. The Nation's annual celebrations on February 26 (Fard's birthday) drew thousands of followers to Chicago. By 1960, the Black Muslims had 50 temples in operation, with membership estimated at 50,000 by the early 1960s. Ten to 30 percent of these were registered followers; thousands more sympathized with the Nation's tenets.

The Nation of Islam was no longer the fringe group that many of its critics believed it to be. Its small businesses now included grocery stores, apartment buildings, factories, farms, cleaning establishments, and repair shops. The combined wealth of these enterprises was estimated at $10 million during the 1950s, and in 1960 the Nation owned half a million dollars' worth of real estate in the Chicago area alone. In 1961 Malcolm X successfully merged his recruitment campaign with the Nation's business efforts by founding *Muhammad Speaks,* a weekly periodical sold by Black Muslims who received a portion of the paper's profits. The newspaper's circulation reached a half million—making it the largest black publication in the country.

The Nation of Islam that Gene Walcott—now named Louis X—joined in 1955 was thus an organization that had enjoyed enormous growth in the 25 years of its existence but one that nonetheless had not yet reached the peak of its influence. However, because its message was specifically aimed at blacks, it was still largely unknown to white Americans. Only a few years later, however, the Nation of Islam would burst into the public spotlight.

5

A NEW
BEGINNING

※

For Louis X, the Nation of Islam provided a mission—to inspire and uplift his fellow African Americans—and a platform from which to do so. Before long, the enthusiastic follower of the Messenger was appointed a captain in the Fruit of Islam, the Nation's security force, and stationed in Boston. In May 1957, only a few months later, Louis was appointed minister of the city's Temple Number Eleven, which Malcolm X had established four years earlier.

A college dropout himself, Louis X found it difficult at first to empathize with the college-educated blacks who were attracted to the teachings of Elijah Muhammad. He had even greater difficulty understanding the needs of the former convicts, prostitutes, drug addicts, and other outcasts who were also drawn to the Nation of Islam. Malcolm X, a self-educated man who was now minister of Temple Number Seven in New York, would frequently travel to Boston to speak at Louis X's temple. He reassured the young minister that teaching the truths of the Nation of Islam did not require an advanced academic degree. The two ministers became close friends, and with Malcolm's assistance and moral

Louis Farrakhan, dressed in the uniform of the Fruit of Islam, addresses a gathering of Black Muslims.

support, Louis managed over the next five years to triple his temple's membership.

Residents of Roxbury who had known Louis X as Gene Walcott were amazed at the transformation from lively musician to somber religious leader. Many attended Nation of Islam gatherings out of curiosity about the neighborhood boy who had grown up and returned home, and most were surprised to discover that Black Muslim meetings did not include the vibrant music or energetic hand-clapping of their Baptist or Episcopalian services.

But the Charmer in Louis X had not disappeared. Shortly after converting to the Nation of Islam, he wrote and recorded a song entitled "A White Man's Heaven Is a Black Man's Hell." Over 10 minutes long, the unusual song mixes a bright calypso rhythm with dire lyrics that proclaim the prophecies of Elijah Muhammad and warn of the demise of the white man:

> We now can stand up
> The whole world to tell
> Our God has come to give us heaven
> And to take the devil
> into hell. . . .
>
> The black man everywhere
> is on the rise. . . .
> The whole black world has
> their eyes on you.
> To see what the so-called Negro
> is going to do.
> So, my friend, it's easy to tell
> Our unity will give the white man hell.

Louis's angry message rang true for many African Americans who had experienced racial discrimination, and the song's upbeat rhythm was popular with listeners. The record sold well, and for years it was played in Nation of Islam restaurants across the country as an effective recruiting tool. In 1959 a man named Lonnie Cross stopped at a restaurant in

Buffalo, New York, with some friends and heard the tune for the first time. The words immediately "made sense" to the young men: "They told the truth," Cross later said. The following year, he heard Elijah Muhammad speak in Atlanta and joined the Nation of Islam. In 1963, Cross—now named Abdul Alim Shabazz—became minister of the Nation's temple in Washington, D.C.

Although music and dancing were forbidden to Black Muslims, Elijah Muhammad permitted Louis X to continue spreading his message through song because "A White Man's Heaven" drew hundreds of

"Our unity will give the white man hell": Farrakhan (then known as Louis X) recorded this calypso-style single, "A White Man's Heaven Is a Black Man's Hell," shortly after joining the Nation of Islam.

By the early 1960s Malcolm X, Farrakhan's mentor, had become the Nation of Islam's most powerful spokesman.

new members to the Nation. The Messenger even allowed his young minister to perform during the Nation of Islam's New Year's Day ceremony in 1958.

Encouraged by this success, Louis recorded a second song a few years later called "Look at My Chains," and wrote two musical allegory plays, *The Trial* and *Orgena* ("a negro" spelled backwards), which toured together in major American cities, including New York, Chicago, Detroit, and Washington, D.C. Like "A White Man's Heaven," the plays—in which Louis himself appeared—focus on the wrongs perpetrated against blacks by whites, who are called "the greatest liar[s] on earth." In *The Trial*, a jury of blacks finds all white people guilty of sinning against their race throughout history, while

Orgena portrays the problems of modern blacks as the result of their having been "kidnapped" from their own noble and ancient culture.

Despite—or perhaps because of—the popularity of such productions, Elijah Muhammad eventually put a stop to Louis X's creative endeavors. "Brother," he asked him, "do you want to be a song-and-dance man or do you want to be my minister?" For Louis X, the choice was clear: "I want to be your minister, dear Holy Apostle," he replied. From that time, Louis ceased writing songs and plays and adopted the somber demeanor of his mentor, Malcolm X.

Aside from Black Muslim restrictions on music and dance, Elijah Muhammad may have had other reasons for restraining the musical enthusiasm of his disciple. While Louis X was writing and performing, Malcolm X had risen to prominence among the Nation's leaders, and his sharp, unyielding rhetoric against the "white devil" had begun to attract the attention not only of disillusioned African Americans but of white Americans as well. Elijah Muhammad may have felt that Louis's musical efforts were diluting the powerful effects of Malcolm's more solemn message of black self-reliance and rebellion.

The Nation of Islam first gained widespread attention in April 1957, when a Black Muslim named Hinton Johnson was severely beaten by policemen and detained in a Harlem jail. Immediately upon hearing the news, Malcolm X and 100 Fruit of Islam members marched to the Harlem police station, drawing hundreds of curious followers along the way. Concerned that a race riot would erupt, the police at the precinct station urged Malcolm X to help break up the angry crowd, which now numbered more than 800. He refused to comply until the police guaranteed that the prisoner would receive medical treatment and that the men who assaulted him would be punished. Only after the police assured him that they would do what he asked did Malcolm turn to his followers. Without a word, he flicked his hands, and the crowd dispersed. A nearby policeman watched in amazement. "No man should have that much power," he said.

Having gained a larger audience of blacks—and the attention of whites—Malcolm X escalated his antiwhite attacks. The Nation of Islam was thrust into the national spotlight in 1959 when an African-American journalist, Louis Lomax, produced a television documentary on the Black Muslims. Pleased at the prospect of national media coverage and convinced that such extensive publicity would help to promote the Nation's teachings, Elijah Muhammad had sanctioned the project.

But the report was far different from what the Black Muslims expected. Entitled "The Hate That Hate Produced," the TV program, narrated by Mike Wallace, vividly portrayed the Nation's deep resentment toward white society and presented graphic evidence that a storm of rebellion was gathering in the black ghettos of America. Many white viewers were shocked and horrified to learn of the intense bitterness that African Americans felt toward them, and they were appalled to hear that blacks thought them the embodiment of evil. The scorching words of Malcolm X and the footage of Louis X playing the role of a prosecutor of whites in *The Trial* filled them with fear, guilt, and distaste.

During the 1950s and '60s, racial discrimination became one of the most hotly debated issues in America. While Malcolm X was delivering his fiery message of black separatism to the urban poor in the North, a young minister named Martin Luther King Jr. was forging a different path to black independence by leading a boycott of segregated bus services in Montgomery, Alabama. Throughout the South, civil rights organizations such as the Southern Christian Leadership Conference (SCLC) and the Congress on Racial Equality (CORE) were challenging racial segregation in public schools and theaters, in restaurants and rest rooms, on trains and buses. Despite their philosophy of nonviolent protest, civil rights activists often met with brutal retaliation from police officers and white supremacists. Nevertheless, many were beginning to feel that their actions could erode racial discrimination in the South.

But Malcolm X openly scorned the goals and methods of such protesters. "You can sit down next to white folks—on the toilet," he remarked, belittling recent rulings outlawing segregated rest rooms. He was contemptuous of African Americans and whites who sought racial integration and harmony. To Malcolm X, the idea of asking whites to grant basic human rights to those who should already have them was deplorable. Instead, like Marcus Garvey and Wallace Fard before them, Malcolm X and Elijah Muhammad began calling for a separate state for blacks within the United States. "The Negro must think in terms of bettering himself, and this he can only do by thinking in terms of his own black civilization," Muhammad told a *New York Times* reporter in 1963. Opposing Martin Luther King's peaceful protests and his vision of a fully integrated society, Malcolm X called on African Americans to fight for their constitutional rights and to defend themselves without hesitation when attacked—"bullet for bullet," if necessary.

Such heated exhortations unsettled and angered not only a great number of whites but also many blacks, especially those who adhered to King's philosophy of peaceful revolution. Three months after the Hinton Johnson incident, Roy Wilkins, the executive secretary for the NAACP, officially condemned the Nation's radical stance. "For years the NAACP has been opposed to white extremists for preaching hatred of Negro people," he declared, "and we are equally opposed to Negro extremists preaching against white people simply for the sake of

Roy Wilkins, executive secretary of the National Association for the Advancement of Colored People, testifies before a U.S. Senate subcommittee considering civil rights legislation. Mainstream civil rights organizations like the NAACP, which believed that African Americans could achieve equality through nonviolent protest, often found themselves at odds with the more militant Black Muslims.

Strange bedfellows: American Nazi Party leader George Lincoln Rockwell (center, reading newspaper) and a group of followers at a 1961 Nation of Islam rally in Washington, D.C. Rockwell and Elijah Muhammad had found common ground in their mutual opposition to racially mixed marriages.

whiteness." The Nation of Islam, however, not only continued to advocate separatism but also opposed the Christian philosophy of turning the other cheek, maintaining that such behavior fostered self-hatred—the greatest crime possible against oneself and one's own kind.

The Nation of Islam's concept of a separate state for African Americans also appealed to those who desired not to see African Americans attain equality but to remove them from the country entirely. In June 1961, George Lincoln Rockwell, head of the white supremacist American Nazi Party, attended a Nation of Islam rally in Washington, D.C., where he announced his support of the Nation's rule against racially mixed marriages. The following year, Elijah Muhammad invited Rockwell to the Nation's annual Savior's Day convention in Chicago. African-American leaders and those who did not espouse the Nation's teachings were horrified. Rockwell, who had once referred to blacks as "the lowest scum of humanity," was now seeking a relationship with a black organization. The mere suggestion of a link between the Nation of Islam and white supremacists was abhorrent to most blacks.

Around the same time, Elijah Muhammad's health began to fail, and Malcolm X increasingly became the focus for journalists and television crews when they needed a statement from the Black Muslims. Always smartly dressed, with a stately bearing and a gift for blazing rhetoric, Malcolm X was an imposing figure. He always dutifully advised the media to consult Muhammad directly on questions regarding the Nation of Islam, but the Messenger was a small, soft-spoken man who lacked the commanding presence of his disciple, so the media continued to spotlight Malcolm.

In 1962, Muhammad named Malcolm X the official spokesperson of the Nation of Islam by appointing him national minister. Although Muhammad retained control over the Nation, Malcolm X was now formally recognized not only as acting head of the movement, but also as heir apparent to the Messenger. Not long after the appointment, Muhammad took the advice of his doctor and moved from Chicago to Phoenix, Arizona.

Trouble arose within the Nation's ranks soon after Elijah Muhammad's departure. Malcolm X's appointment sparked resentment among other Black Muslim officers, especially John Ali, the Nation's head of public relations, and Raymond Sharieff, Muhammad's son-in-law and the head of the Fruit of Islam. Malcolm began hearing insinuations that he had taken advantage of Muhammad's ill health to seize power from him. Soon, he began to suspect that other Black Muslim leaders were turning the Messenger against him.

6

"THE DIE IS SET"

❦

Muhammad's absence from Chicago ultimately created a split in the Nation of Islam's center of authority. The negative media attention and the heightened FBI surveillance of the Nation led many Black Muslim officials to insist on presenting a more moderate public image. They thought it was important to focus on Black Muslim economic programs and religious teachings rather than emphasize the virulently antiwhite sentiments expressed by Malcolm X.

Antagonism among the Nation's officials increased in April 1962, after a confrontation between Black Muslims and Los Angeles police left one member dead and 12 others wounded. A furious Malcolm X vowed to retaliate by attacking the police. Elijah Muhammad and other leaders of the Nation overruled him.

Publicly, Malcolm agreed with the Nation's official decision. Privately, however, he was disappointed by Muhammad's reaction to the violence, and he expressed his frustration over the Nation's increasingly passive responses to blatant police brutality. At the same time, many young members who had been inspired and recruited by the charismatic national

Malcolm X speaks with members of the news media in early 1964, shortly after his fateful decision to break with the Nation of Islam.

Holding their daughters by Elijah Muhammad, Evelyn Williams and Lucille Rosary meet with their lawyer. Muhammad's admission of adultery with his former secretaries capped Malcolm X's disillusionment with the Messenger and precipitated his split with the Nation of Islam.

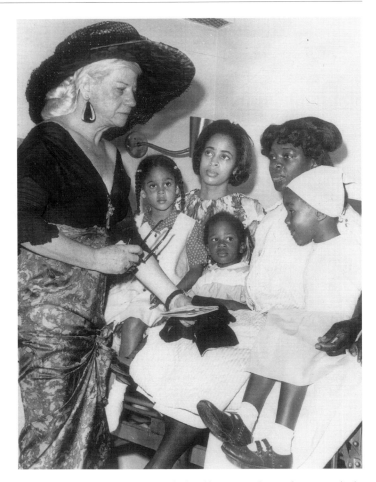

leader also began to feel disillusioned, and many left the Nation of Islam.

Malcolm X also continued to find fault with the nonviolent protest methods of other opponents of prejudice. By the mid-1960s civil rights groups had achieved a number of significant victories, among them the passage of the Civil Rights Act of 1964 and the Economic Opportunity Act. But to Malcolm, legal reforms did not begin to address the day-to-day problems of African Americans. Citing outbreaks of racial violence in Nashville, Birmingham, Atlanta, and Albany, he claimed that the country's racial unrest was still potent enough to explode at any moment into widespread rioting.

Similarly, civil rights leaders objected to the Nation of Islam's official response to racial violence. While many Americans were risking their lives in pursuit of civil rights for African Americans, the Nation of Islam—despite Malcolm X's strong rhetoric—remained a conservative organization that seemed more concerned with establishing a black homeland than with securing political equality.

This criticism was not lost on Malcolm X. After the 1962 police attacks on Black Muslims, he had concluded that neither integration nor black separatism alone would improve the plight of African Americans. In his public addresses, he began to emphasize political involvement over religious and moral concerns, and he appealed to Elijah Muhammad to advocate a more active protest role for the Nation of Islam.

Muhammad refused, insisting upon stressing the traditional Black Muslim teaching of complete segregation. As always, Malcolm obeyed the Messenger's orders. But his changing views about the Nation of Islam's mission were no secret, and they led to further controversy among Black Muslim officials. Finally, Elijah Muhammad took steps to silence Malcolm.

Believing that his national minister was attempting to seize his position, Elijah Muhammad relieved Malcolm X of his duties as editor of the Nation's newspaper, *Muhammad Speaks*; its staff members were instructed to limit coverage of his activities. In addition, the Messenger forbade Malcolm to appear on television news broadcasts.

But Malcolm X's punishment and his desire to redirect the Nation's focus were pushed aside in July 1963, when two former secretaries of Elijah Muhammad brought paternity suits against the Messenger, claiming that he was the father of their four children. Adultery is a grave violation of Black Muslim doctrine, and the news shook Malcolm's faith to its core. When he questioned the two women, Malcolm not only heard evidence to support their charges but also learned of the Messenger's conviction that he had turned against him.

Stunned, Malcolm X confided in his closest friend, Louis X, whom he called "little brother." To Malcolm's surprise, Louis seemed unfazed by the legal accusations, and his faith in Muhammad remained unshaken. "All praise is due to Allah," Louis replied serenely. When Malcolm asked Louis to be silent about the news of Muhammad's indiscretions, Louis replied that he would tell no one—except the Messenger himself. Malcolm decided to confront Elijah Muhammad first.

He was even more shocked when the Messenger admitted that the charges against him were true. Muhammad claimed that he was merely "fulfilling prophecy" and compared himself to the biblical David and Noah, who had committed similar offenses. Matters worsened when Malcolm tried to warn

Malcolm X in Egypt after his 1964 hajj, or pilgrimage, to Mecca. That journey led him to convert to Orthodox Islam and change his name to El Hajj Malik El-Shabazz, to reevaluate his views on whites, and to open up his Muslim Mosque to believers of all races.

other Black Muslim officials to prepare for press reaction to the lawsuits. Later, it became clear that a number of the Nation's officials had long been aware of Elijah Muhammad's infidelities—Farrakhan himself has since admitted to knowledge of Muhammad's affairs. Nevertheless, Malcolm was accused of spreading vicious lies about the Nation's spiritual leader, and his words were received as further evidence that he had turned against the Messenger.

The rift between Malcolm X and Elijah Muhammad became irreparable after President John Kennedy was assassinated on November 22, 1963. Muhammad, aware of Kennedy's immense popularity and fearful of violence against Black Muslims should they speak of the murder, enjoined his ministers not to discuss the event. But on December 1, after delivering a public address, Malcolm was asked by reporters to comment on the president's death. He replied that white America was being repaid for fostering an atmosphere of hatred against blacks. "Being an old farm boy myself," Malcolm said, smiling, "chickens coming home to roost never did make me sad. They've always made me glad."

Malcolm's careless statement provoked a national uproar and further condemnation of the Nation of Islam, whose beliefs and practices were by this time under heavy attack. Angered by Malcolm's disobedience, Muhammad suspended him from his duties as national minister for 90 days and forbade him to speak to the press. But Malcolm would not be silent. He continued to speak to reporters, at times revealing clues about the struggle for power in the Nation's ranks.

A month later, Malcolm X was charged with conspiring to overthrow Elijah Muhammad and was removed from his position as minister of New York's Temple Number Seven. At the same time, Elijah excommunicated his son Wallace for his alleged complicity in Malcolm's plot to overthrow him. Not long

"The die is set, and Malcolm shall not escape. . . . Such a man as Malcolm is worthy of death," thundered Farrakhan in a speech denouncing his former mentor. Three months later Malcolm X was murdered.

after, Malcolm learned of several plots against his life by Black Muslims. Although he had received numerous death threats before, the idea that other Black Muslims would be willing to kill him was devastating.

Finally, on March 8, 1964, Malcolm announced that he was leaving the Nation of Islam and establishing his own movement called Muslim Mosque, Incorporated. He vowed that he would continue to advocate militancy against racial oppression.

Only a few weeks after establishing the Muslim Mosque, Malcolm went on a spiritual pilgrimage, or hajj, to Mecca, where he began to see traditional Islam in a new light. He met European Muslims with blue eyes and blond hair who were as reverent as their darker counterparts, and he concluded that whites are not inherently evil, as Black Muslim teaching claimed. Rather, they are influenced by racist society to act in evil ways. His views on race and religion were forever changed. In June 1964, Malcolm X converted to Orthodox Islam, changing his name to El Hajj Malik El-Shabazz.

Upon his return to the United States, Malcolm opened his Muslim Mosque to all followers, regardless of race, declaring that "black nationalism" was not a product of the Nation of Islam but was taught "in the Christian church," in civil rights organizations, "in Muslim meetings," and even "where nothing but atheists and agnostics come together." To Malcolm, black nationalism did not mean hatred for other races; it meant only that African Americans were responsible for controlling the politics of their own communities.

Denounced as a "turncoat" whom "we should destroy" by Black Muslim officials, Malcolm was vilified even by his own brothers, Philbert and Reginald, who had introduced Malcolm to the Nation of Islam during his imprisonment. At a press conference, Philbert read a statement calling his brother a "wayward" and "cunning" schemer who would "do anything" to keep himself in the public eye.

None of the Nation's ministers was as vigorous or public in his condemnation of Malcolm X as Louis X. In a three-part series in *Muhammad Speaks*, Louis branded the man who once called him "little brother" a lying, jealous, and greedy traitor. Malcolm, said Louis X, had "benefited and profited most from [the Messenger's] generosity," yet had "played the hypocrite on both sides" by pretending to be a follower of Elijah while pandering to the white man. And then Louis X made a statement that plagues him to this day:

> Only those who wish to be led to hell, or to their doom, will follow Malcolm. The die is set, and Malcolm shall not escape. . . . Such a man as Malcolm is

worthy of death, and would have met death if it had not been for Muhammad's confidence in Allah for victory over his enemies.

Three months later, on February 21, 1965, Malcolm X was assassinated as he stood at a podium in Harlem's Audubon Ballroom on West 166th Street. Although Elijah Muhammad and the Nation of Islam denied involvement in the attack, Malcolm X's assailants were later identified as Black Muslims.

Many who remembered Louis X's violent words would link him with the murder. Years later, Louis Farrakhan recalled his actions on the day of Malcolm's murder. He had just delivered a lecture at the Nation's temple in Newark, New Jersey, and was in a Black Muslim restaurant across the street from the temple when he heard of Malcolm's death over the radio. He left the restaurant and walked the streets, he said,

> reflecting on this man who was my teacher, my mentor. Though I disagreed vehemently with Malcolm's characterization of the honorable Elijah Muhammad, I was not happy that such a man was murdered.

Farrakhan continues to disavow direct involvement in the assassination. However, he has recently acknowledged that his strong denouncements of Malcolm X "helped to create an atmosphere" of condemnation and anger that led to the killing. And in an interview with Barbara Walters on ABC TV's *20/20* in 1994, he declared, "Today . . . Malcolm would be so much more valuable to us alive."

At times, Louis Farrakhan expresses a peculiar mix of resentment and respect for his early mentor. Although he still condemns Malcolm for "betraying" Elijah Muhammad, he occasionally acknowledges his talents as an orator and recruiter. In 1993 Arthur Magida, a journalist and biographer of Farrakhan, captured the minister on tape as he discussed Malcolm X and his role in the Nation of Islam. "Malcolm was a pimp, a thief, a hustler, a dope user, a dope

Mortally wounded, Malcolm X is wheeled away from the Audubon Ballroom after being shot by assassins later identified as Black Muslims, February 21, 1965.

seller, a disrespecter of women," Farrakhan declared.

> He was this before he met Elijah Muhammad. That's when the world became acquainted with Malcolm X. Was Malcolm the deceived one? . . . What did Malcolm X have that somebody could trick him out of? He didn't have money. He didn't have fame. He didn't have sense. When he left Elijah Muhammad, he wasn't wealthy, but he certainly was famous. And he certainly had plenty of knowledge. He only went through eighth grade, but no college graduate of white America could defeat Malcolm in argument or debate. So Malcolm didn't come out a loser.

Nor did Farrakhan. Shortly after the death of Malcolm X, Louis X was appointed minister of the prestigious Temple Number Seven in New York, where Malcolm had preached for years. Thirteen years later, Louis Farrakhan would become the leader of the Nation of Islam.

7

TERROR

— ❧ —

Louis X had not been minister of the New York temple for long before the Nation's detractors—including the FBI—began charging him and other New York officials of the Nation of Islam with financial corruption. In April 1968, FBI agents anonymously distributed to nearly 300 members of Temple Number Seven a pamphlet—designed in comic-book style, according to an FBI memo, to "appeal to a generally uneducated audience"—that detailed the alleged "high living" and corruption of the Temple's ministers. The rumors appeared valid to some observers, who noted that Louis X led a relatively lavish life, complete with finely tailored clothing, expensive cars, and a maid for his nine-room home in East Elmhurst, the predominantly white New York suburb where he lived with his wife and seven of their nine children.

Louis X was never accused or convicted of any wrongdoing; nevertheless, Elijah Muhammad sent the supreme captain of the Fruit of Islam to New York to look into the FBI's charges. After a stern admonishment by Muhammad's emissary, Temple Number Seven officials were ordered by Elijah Muhammad to be more stringent in keeping financial records.

Charges of financial corruption were only part of more widespread problems developing within the Nation of Islam. By the early 1970s Elijah Muhammad, suffering from severe bronchial asthma and

As Elijah Muhammad's control slipped in the early 1970s, Black Muslims battled police—and one another. Here an arsonist's work consumes a Nation of Islam temple in Harlem.

A crowd mills around Temple Number Seven in Harlem, April 14, 1972. Earlier, a clash between temple members and police had turned into a full-scale riot. Farrakhan's efforts to quell the disturbance drew the praise of the New York Times.

now permanently residing in Phoenix, was losing his firm grip on the organization. Only rarely did he visit the Nation's headquarters in Chicago, where rumors about his successor had begun circulating among officials.

The Nation of Islam, now lacking a strong center of power, was beginning to weaken. In the years following the death of Malcolm X, quarreling among Black Muslim leaders and reports of violence against those who opposed the Nation drastically reduced the organization's numbers. Others began to question the truth of Muhammad's teachings and to dispute his theology; many of these people formed splinter groups, which also drew followers away from the Nation. Some members who left on their own even approached the FBI out of fear that the Nation would attempt to punish them for "desertion," as it seemed to have done to Malcolm X and other former Black Muslims.

The unrest that plagued the Nation of Islam mirrored the discontent and anger felt by African Americans across the country. Increasingly desperate for change, disaffected blacks expressed their frustration in riots. This disquiet, coupled with the advances made by civil rights activists, led many Black Muslims to question the organization's nonactivist stance. But Muhammad steadfastly refused to attract further attention to the Nation of Islam by involving it in active protests against racial discrimination. As a result, the Nation's powerful hold on black public opinion began to wane.

Violence within the Nation itself reached a critical point in October 1971, when Muhammad's son-in-law and chief bodyguard, Fruit of Islam head Raymond Sharieff, was shot and wounded near the office of *Muhammad Speaks*. Three months later, in apparent retribution for the attack, two members of a Black Muslim dissident group were murdered. In December 1972, a guard at the Nation's Salaam

Restaurant in Chicago was killed.

Louis Farrakhan was not immune from the internal battles and jealousies swirling within the Nation's Chicago offices. Many of those closest to Elijah Muhammad, including his sons, did not trust Farrakhan. Pointing to the success of a New York rally called the Black Family Day Bazaar, to which Farrakhan had attracted 70,000 attendees, they alleged that he was becoming too powerful and would attempt to wrest control of the Nation from Elijah, as they believed Malcolm X had done. They even had a nickname for the smooth-talking but distrusted minister: "Velvet Mouth."

In 1972, the simmering hostilities between law enforcement and Nation of Islam members came to a head. That spring, two New York policemen burst into the Harlem temple headed by Louis X (whose name Elijah Muhammad had recently changed to Louis Farrakhan) and rushed upstairs to the second floor, claiming that they had received a distress call from a detective who was "in trouble" there. They were met by angry Black Muslims, who tried to evict them. Other members locked the entrances to the temple to keep out police reinforcements, who had arrived on the scene wearing bulletproof vests and armed with automatic weapons.

Before long, the disturbance became a full-scale riot. More than 1,000 blacks gathered outside the temple, throwing rocks and bottles at white policemen and setting a police car on fire, while police helicopters circled the area and the press looked on. For three hours, the chaos continued. At some point during the riot, however, Louis Farrakhan took action to quell the disturbance. Jumping on top of a parked car, he shouted to the rioters, "This is our community and we're minding our own business. But every brother and sister here, just be cool. Don't let anyone provoke you."

Farrakhan's courageous efforts to restore peace

were praised by the Nation of Islam. "This wasn't facile," a Black Muslim official later declared. "This wasn't entertainment. He was no jive dude. He was committed to 'the struggle.'" In its April 17 report on the disturbance, the *New York Times* hailed Farrakhan as having "long before gained [a reputation] for dependability in Harlem."

In 1973, the Nation of Islam exploded in bloodshed. In January, seven Hanafi Muslims—part of a dissident group that had broken from the Nation— were murdered in Washington, D.C. Presumably targeting Hamaas Abdul Khaalis, the Hanafi leader, the assassins instead drowned three infants, fatally shot Khaalis's 10- and 25-year-old sons and two other Hanafi members in the head, and shot and wounded the mother of two of the infants and Khaalis's 23-year-old daughter (the women survived). Juries eventually convicted seven Nation of Islam members from Philadelphia of the murders, which were apparently

At a news conference the day after the riot at Temple Number Seven, Farrakhan demands an apology from New York City's mayor and police commissioner, saying that the police had acted like "brute beasts" in breaking into the mosque.

James Shabazz (above), minister of Temple Number Twenty-five in Newark, New Jersey, was one of the victims of the Black Muslims' intragroup violence. Shabazz was gunned down as he got out of his car in September 1973.

committed in revenge for Khaalis's having called Elijah Muhammad a false prophet.

James Price, one of the alleged attackers, was called upon to testify against his coconspirators. But the day before he was scheduled to appear in court, he apparently heard a radio address by Louis Farrakhan, who delivered a chilling warning to "those of you who would be used as an instrument of wicked government against our rise." Beware, advised Farrakhan,

> because when the government is tired of you, they're going to dump you back into the laps of your people. And though Elijah Muhammad is a merciful man and will say, "Come in," and forgive you, yet in the ranks of the black people today there are younger men and women who have no forgiveness in them for traitors and stool pigeons. And they will execute you, as soon as your identity is known.

Price refused to testify; the following day, he was found hanging in his prison cell.

Four months after the Washington murders, Hakim Jamal, the head of a group called the Malcolm X Foundation, was killed in his Roxbury home by five gunmen who were later identified as Black Muslims. This too was thought to be retribution for Jamal's criticism of Elijah Muhammad.

In September 1973, James Shabazz, the minister of the Nation of Islam's Temple Number Twenty-five in Newark, New Jersey, was gunned down by two black men while getting out of his car. Three members of Shabazz's temple kidnapped a black police officer the next day in an attempt to gain information on the murder investigation. (The officer was released after two days.)

It is not known whether Elijah Muhammad, who had become quite frail, had a clear idea of the brutality growing within the ranks of the Nation. His son Wallace believed that his father was unaware of most of the violence. "I think he was deceived," Wallace said of his father in 1977. "He was told that nobody was getting whipped, except those who attacked us." Throughout this tumultuous period, however, Elijah Muhammad exhorted his followers to refrain from violence and crime: "Just take that which God has given you and make something out of it. . . . You go to war with no man! No! You go to war with yourself."

But Louis Farrakhan was promoting a different message. The week after James Shabazz was killed, Farrakhan delivered an extraordinarily harsh Sunday sermon, which he called "The Murderer of a Muslim." In it, he declared incorrectly that "It is written in the holy Quran that whosoever kills a Muslim, he must be killed." He went on:

> We are not trying to say . . . [that we are] taking the law into our own hands. No, we are not permitted to do that. But we are taking the law of God into our hands that God has put into our hands. . . .
>
> We are not an evil people. We are lovers of life and we respect the sacredness of life . . . but he who did not respect the sacredness of the life of [James Shabazz] . . . what right do we have to respect a life like that?

Farrakhan continued by describing how such people should be punished: "Smite them at the back of the neck. . . . Take off their heads since it is in their heads that the thought of evil was hatched."

Farrakhan's denouncement, broadcast over the radio as were all his sermons, may have inspired further bloodshed. A week after the sermon was delivered, two young members of the Newark temple were shot to death, and in October, two more former members were found in a nearby park. They had been decapitated, their heads found about four miles away, near Shabazz's residence.

A short time later, the Newark police arrested 11 members of a group called the New World Order of Islam, a dissident faction of the Newark temple that had been feuding with Shabazz over his conservative management. After the arrests, the killings finally ceased.

8

TRANSFORMATION

❧

Although only a small number of the Nation's members engaged in violence, such incidents garnered national media attention. Less publicized was the extraordinary shift in Elijah Muhammad's philosophy regarding the future of the Nation of Islam. In stark contrast to years of teaching about the demise of the hated white man, Muhammad's teachings moved closer to the beliefs of Orthodox Islam, and he tempered his abhorrence of whites. In his last major public address, which he delivered on Savior's Day in 1974, the Messenger urged his followers to respect not only their fellow Muslims but whites as well. "I say that the Black man in North America has nobody to blame but himself," he declared, reversing his earlier view that whites were to blame for the condition of blacks in America. "If [the black man] respects himself and will do for himself, his once slavemaster will come and respect him and help him to do something for self."

Less than a year later, Elijah Muhammad was hospitalized, and on February 25, 1975—the day before Savior's Day—the 77-year-old Messenger died

"A legend in his time, more than surpassing in dynamism and charisma all the claims for the late Malcolm X," wrote the magazine Sepia *in 1975 in describing Louis Farrakhan, the Nation of Islam's rising star.*

Frail and sickly, Elijah Muhammad delivers a Savior's Day address. In the months leading up to Muhammad's death in February 1975, Farrakhan appeared to be the clear choice to succeed the Messenger. In the end, however, Elijah Muhammad's son Wallace was appointed Supreme Minister of the Nation of Islam.

of heart failure. The following day, the Nation of Islam announced the appointment of Elijah's son, Wallace Muhammad, as Supreme Minister of the Nation of Islam.

Wallace Muhammad seemed an unlikely choice to succeed his father. He had been expelled from the Nation in 1964 for allegedly plotting against Elijah Muhammad by giving sensitive information to Malcolm X. Angry at his expulsion, he had accused the Nation—and even some of his own relatives—of moral and religious bankruptcy. Although he "repented" and was welcomed back after Malcolm's assassination, he was excommunicated twice more—in 1965 and in 1974—before finally rejoining his father's administration.

Louis Farrakhan almost certainly had heard hints of Wallace's appointment before the Messenger's death. Nevertheless, the choice seemed to come as a surprise to him and to many other top officials of the Nation, who believed that Farrakhan's dedication and swift rise to power were definite indications that he would be chosen to lead the Nation.

Though stunned and disturbed by the appointment, Farrakhan resolved to present a united front with Wallace Muhammad. At the Savior's Day convention where the announcement was made, Farrakhan praised Wallace, calling his appointment the "will of God" and resolving to remain faithful "to the only man I ever knew that was worthy of being faithful to." Farrakhan vowed to "submit and yield and give of myself and all that I have and within my power to see that the work of Messenger Muhammad is carried on to its completion by the work of his son."

Despite such assurances of continuity, the Nation of Islam would undergo dramatic reforms under Wallace Muhammad. The first came shortly after his appointment, when he abandoned the Nation's traditional demand for a separate black state within America. The Nation's mission had changed, Wallace said, from an organization dedicated to black upliftment to one that had helped to create a black consciousness and thus had no reason to separate itself from the rest of the world. Echoing the belief that Malcolm X had reached late in life—that whites are not intrinsically evil—the Supreme Minister declared that whites were "fully human" and welcome to join the Nation of Islam.

In addition to doctrinal changes, Wallace relaxed the Nation's strict dress code (jackets, bow ties, and clean-shaven faces for men, neck-to-ankle dresses and veils for women), reshaped Savior's Day as

Less than two years after taking over the leadership of the Nation of Islam, Wallace Muhammad (at right) declared the organization defunct, replacing it with a nonracial, Orthodox Islamic group called the World Community of al-Islam in the West. Farrakhan, claiming to be the true spiritual heir to Elijah Muhammad, broke with Wallace Muhammad and set about resurrecting the Nation of Islam.

"Ethnic Survival Week," and renamed the Nation's newspaper the *Bilalian News*, offering articles on secular subjects and dropping the list of political directives that had appeared in every issue of *Muhammad Speaks*.

These changes were followed by even more surprising financial reforms. In 1976, Wallace Muhammad publicly disclosed that the Nation's net worth—until then a closely guarded secret—was $46 million. He began selling off the movement's properties in an effort to improve its deteriorating financial situation. He revised the pay scale of his ministers to avoid competition and corruption and removed all of them from involvement in the Nation's remaining business enterprises.

Most startling of all, especially to Louis Farrakhan, was the Supreme Minister's declaration that Elijah Muhammad would no longer be considered the Messenger of Allah; he was simply a wise man who had brought the Quran to African Americans. Nor was Wallace Fard a divine being; he was merely the founder of the Nation of Islam.

Meanwhile, Louis Farrakhan's commanding presence continued to divert attention from the Nation's leader. The magazine *Sepia* summed up black America's fascination with Farrakhan in a May 1975 article:

> He's a better orator than the late Dr. Martin Luther King Jr. He sings better than Marvin Gaye. He's a better writer than Norman Mailer. He dresses better than Walt Frazier. He's more of a diplomat than Henry Kissinger. And he's prettier than [boxer] Muhammad Ali. . . . A legend in his time, more than surpassing in dynamism and charisma all the claims for the late Malcolm X.

Such glowing words of praise did not ingratiate Farrakhan to Wallace Muhammad. But Wallace realized that firing Farrakhan would endanger the stability of his newly reformed organization. Instead, he took steps to reduce the minister's popularity and influence. In June 1975, he removed Farrakhan from his prominent post as head of Temple Number Seven in New York—the same position from which Malcolm X had been removed and which Farrakhan had assumed after Malcolm's assassination. He transferred Farrakhan to Chicago, assigning him to a small temple and naming him his own "special ambassador." The "promotion" was clearly a way for Wallace to keep closer watch over Farrakhan.

Most trying of all for Louis Farrakhan was the Nation's official reversal of its attitude toward

Malcolm X. Previously reviled as a traitor, Farrakhan's former mentor was now revered as a martyr and prophet: Temple Number Seven, which had flourished under Malcolm's leadership, was renamed the Malcolm Shabazz Temple after the man whom Farrakhan had declared "worthy of death." Feeling increasingly marginalized and embittered, Farrakhan began to understand the disillusionment Malcolm X had experienced 10 years earlier. "I turned away from Malcolm," he told an interviewer in 1977:

> Only later did I learn . . . [t]hat I had to walk in his shoes to understand where he was coming from. . . . to be scorned by my own Muslim brothers. To be suspect because of a growing popularity, as was Malcolm. To be undermined and vilified as was Malcolm. The only thing I don't want to repeat is the end of Malcolm.

On October 18, 1976, Wallace Muhammad declared the Nation of Islam extinct. In its place, he instituted a nonracial, nonpolitical group called the World Community of al-Islam in the West (WCIW), which embraced Orthodox Islam and welcomed all people, regardless of color. The last vestige of the Nation of Islam, the private security force known as the Fruit of Islam, was abolished shortly thereafter.

The strain of publicly supporting Wallace Muhammad's sweeping changes while remaining privately faithful to Elijah Muhammad's teachings eventually became too great for Louis Farrakhan. By this time, news of a split between the two leaders had reached the media. Persistent rumors of death threats against Farrakhan were checked by Wallace, but Farrakhan told a *Chicago Tribune* reporter, "I am not welcomed in the World Community of al-Islam in the West and I know it."

In December 1977, in an eerie replay of Malcolm X's decision, Farrakhan announced that he was severing all ties with Wallace Muhammad and the WCIW. God had awakened him, he declared, and he had returned to his post as an upholder of Elijah

Muhammad's philosophy of black separatism and strict moral and religious discipline.

In March 1978, Farrakhan announced that he was reviving the Nation of Islam and its doctrines. Declaring himself the true successor of Elijah Muhammad, Farrakhan cited several conversations with the Messenger: "You can sit over the Nation as the father when I'm gone," he had presumably told his faithful minister. "As Allah made me to take his place among the people, I am making you to take my place." He claimed that Elijah had even predicted his fall from grace but had also told Farrakhan that he would regain his power and influence and would assume leadership of the Nation of Islam.

Under his direction, Farrakhan now declared, a new Nation, complete with its traditional doctrinal truths and myths, its newspaper, its security force—and its property—would rise to its former strength.

9

FORGING
A NEW NATION

Louis Farrakhan's revival of the original Nation of Islam was largely unchallenged by Wallace Muhammad and the WCIW. Despite having been excommunicated from the Nation several times, Wallace, like Farrakhan, claimed that he was the spiritual heir of Elijah Muhammad.

Nevertheless, both men were mindful of the tragic outcome of Malcolm X's break with the Nation of Islam. Wallace urged his followers to avoid public criticism of Farrakhan and to refrain from protesting his meetings. Thus, although the break was far from amicable—accusations of fraud and heresy were lobbed from both sides—it did not result in violence.

For his part, Louis Farrakhan made no overt attempts to divert members from the WCIW. However, he was oddly successful in drawing members of Elijah Muhammad's own extensive family to his movement, including the Messenger's six common-law wives and the 13 children they bore him. Of these, one son, Kamal, became the Nation's national secretary; two others, Abdullah and Ishmael, became ministers.

A 15-city tour in 1985 emphasized Farrakhan's commitment to African-American economic progress. Several times during his tenure as leader of the Nation of Islam, Farrakhan has tried to reach beyond his Black Muslim followers to the larger community of African Americans.

Farrakhan realized, however, that without connections to a powerful and established organization his new movement would not survive. In search of financial and political support, he approached leaders of the Black Nationalist movement in Chicago.

An affiliation of African-American groups who advocated racial separatism and the establishment of a black homeland, Black Nationalists emerged from the Black Power movement of the 1960s, which was initiated by African-American political activist Stokely Carmichael. During the 1960s, many Black Nationalists looked to the Nation of Islam not for Elijah Muhammad's religious doctrine and strict authoritarianism, but for the powerful message of separatism delivered by its national minister, Malcolm X. The alliance disintegrated after Malcolm's assassination, in part because of the belief that the Nation had killed its own minister. But most Black Nationalists also began to feel that the Nation was being run like a private business, with little concern for the greater issues facing African Americans outside the organization.

Because of their history with the former Nation of Islam, many Black Nationalists were reluctant to meet with Louis Farrakhan. Among those who finally did was Haki Madhubuti, who had once been a distinguished poet and a follower of Malcolm X, though not a Black Muslim himself.

Farrakhan's goal, as Madhubuti related in his 1994 book *Claiming Earth,* was "to involve the 'Nation' with the larger Black community." He told Madhubuti and other black leaders that although he intended to follow the teachings of Elijah Muhammad, the Messenger had been overly "exclusive and secret." According to Madhubuti, Farrakhan described the new Nation of Islam as "more political . . . less self-righteous and all-knowing, one that would keep its communication lines open and work as part of a Black united front."

Satisfied with Farrakhan's plans for broader solidarity among blacks, a group of about 30 African-American leaders agreed to finance the new Nation of Islam. Farrakhan held his first public assembly as leader of the Nation in the packed auditorium of the Institute of Positive Education, a school run by Madhubuti.

By mortgaging his home, Farrakhan managed to purchase a former funeral home on 79th Street in Chicago, where he later established his first temple. Then, in an effort to gain new adherents, Farrakhan began to travel across the country, delivering lectures and establishing "study groups" that would later blossom into full-fledged Nation of Islam temples.

Only a few years after the new Nation was founded, however, many of those who had agreed to support Farrakhan had become skeptical of the minister's promises to create a more open and democratic organization. Farrakhan had reinstituted not only the philosophy of Elijah Muhammad but also some of the trappings of the old movement. He revived the Fruit of Islam, the Nation's security force, and required body searches of all those who attended his meetings. In 1979, he resuscitated the Nation of Islam's official newspaper, renaming it *The Final Call* after Elijah Muhammad's first periodical of 1934.

Moreover, in the new Black Muslim mythology, Farrakhan continued to maintain that Wallace Fard was Allah, and he elevated Elijah Muhammad—formerly viewed as a messenger of Allah—to the level of a messiah. Feeling that Farrakhan had betrayed them, most of his original backers began to distance themselves from him.

By this time, though, Farrakhan was less needful of such support. His efforts at attracting new members had been fruitful: between 6,000 and 7,000 members attended the new Nation's first Savior's Day in 1981. With success came improved organization and funding: the sporadically published *Final Call* became a monthly in 1983, and in 1986 Farrakhan purchased Elijah Muhammad's former mansion in Hyde Park, New York, for the Nation's headquarters and his family residence. Similarly, Farrakhan also acquired some of the property that Wallace Muhammad had sold off in his effort to reform the WCIW—including Temple Number Two in Chicago, one of the most prized possessions of Elijah Muhammad's Nation of Islam.

Louis Farrakhan's desire to adhere closely to the teachings of Elijah Muhammad was tested during the 1980s. Up to that time, Black Muslims had obeyed Muhammad's injunction against political involvement and therefore did not participate in the electoral process. But 1984 marked a milestone in American politics: for the first time in the country's history, a black man, Jesse Jackson, was campaigning for the presidency of the United States.

A former aide to Martin Luther King Jr., Jackson was also known for having established a program in the 1970s to encourage academic excellence among ghetto youths. Though a black woman, Representative Shirley Chisholm of New York, had become the first African American to seek a presidential nomination, in 1972, Jackson's campaign was a turning point. Many black leaders endorsed the Democrat's idea of creating a "people's platform," a political alliance that transcended racial lines but focused on the economic and social needs of African Americans. Jackson's organization, the National Rainbow Coalition, Inc., sponsored increased voter registration for blacks as a means to establish an African-American power base. Finally, the dream of equal involvement in national politics seemed possible for blacks.

Louis Farrakhan was among those swept up in the excitement. He ardently agreed with Jackson's objective of improving the lives of African Americans and had already publicly endorsed Jackson by traveling

with him to Syria on a mission to free Robert O. Goodman, a black U.S. pilot who had been shot down during a bombing run over Lebanon. On February 9, 1984, Farrakhan marched with 1,000 blacks to Chicago's City Hall, where he registered to vote for the first time. (Although Farrakhan's march was intended to draw attention to the importance of voting, the city recorded only 167 registrations that day.)

Jackson's campaign was already in jeopardy, however. Only six days earlier, the *Washington Post* had run an article discussing the candidate's stormy relationship with Jews. The journalist, Milton Coleman, had included an aside that Jackson made to press representatives in which he referred to Jews in derogatory terms as "Hymies" and to New York City as "Hymietown." The article provoked a tremendous outcry against Jackson, who first denied that he had

With Jesse Jackson looking over their shoulders, Farrakhan and his wife, Betsy, register to vote, February 9, 1984. A bitter, racially charged controversy accompanied Farrakhan's zealous support for Jackson's 1984 presidential bid.

The minister in concert: Farrakhan performs a violin concerto. Some people viewed his 1993 performance of a piece by the Jewish composer Felix Mendelssohn as an overture to Jews.

made the statement, then finally apologized. But it was too late; his comments—and his denial—had seriously damaged his campaign.

In an attempt to support Jackson, Farrakhan assailed and threatened Jewish leaders who condemned him, even going so far as to claim that "Israeli hit squads" were planning to kill the candidate. Using rhetoric that was disturbingly similar to his denunciation of Malcolm X, Farrakhan also attacked Coleman, a black man, as a "no-good filthy traitor" and "a dog" who deserved the ultimate punishment of death.

Coleman himself was frightened enough to seek FBI and police protection; many who were familiar with Farrakhan's oratory, however, believed that his threats were mere hyperbole meant to underscore the Nation of Islam's power and influence. Nine years later, in fact, Farrakhan himself downplayed his own angry statements of 1984, declaring that the threats were "really innocuous and were not intended in any way to harm the Jewish community."

Whatever Farrakhan's intent may have been, his fierce words further compromised Jackson's bid for the presidency and drew unfavorable attention to the Nation of Islam, whose history with Jews was even more turbulent than Jackson's.

Elijah Muhammad had praised the business skills of American Jews and sympathized with the Jewish history of religious persecution. But he was also fiercely critical and suspicious of American Jews because he believed that their support of Israel made them enemies of the Nation's "[Muslim] brothers in the East." Moreover, he disputed the Jewish belief that they are the "chosen people," since Black Muslim theology claims that blacks were the original, chosen race.

Louis Farrakhan continued Muhammad's practice of raging against Jews. Responding to protests against his words, he compared himself to the dictator Adolf Hitler, a "very great man" who also sought to "rais[e his] people up from nothing." At this, even Jesse Jackson, who by this time had all but lost the Democratic nomination, harshly criticized Farrakhan, calling his remarks "unconscionable and reprehensible."

Farrakhan has since made a number of overtures to Jewish Americans and their leaders to repair the rift he created during Jackson's campaign. One of his better-known efforts concerned his continued love for the violin. In 1991, the 58-year-old decided to resume music lessons. His teacher, a Jewish woman named Elaine Skorodkin, professed to be "taken aback" by his request for lessons, but she agreed to it because Farrakhan expressed his belief that "music can transcend differences and he wanted to show his people the beauty of classical music."

On April 18, 1993, Farrakhan ably performed

Felix Mendelssohn's Violin Concerto in Winston-Salem, North Carolina, where he had attended college. Farrakhan knew that Mendelssohn was a Jew, and he told a *New York Times* music critic that the concert provided a means of doing "with music what cannot be undone with words and . . . to undo with music what words have done." Yet after critics complained that he just as easily could have mended the rift with words, Farrakhan claimed that his original intent was simply to play the work of his favorite composer and was not an attempt to avoid responsibility for his anti-Semitic remarks. "It was taken as [an overture to Jews], and I did not reject that, because I thought great good would come of it," he later explained. "I don't do things for publicity. Men of God are not like that. I played Mendelssohn because I love Mendelssohn."

Whatever good may have come from Farrakhan's performance, however, was completely undone the following year at Kean College in New Jersey. There, in November, Nation of Islam official Khallid Abdul Muhammad delivered a scathing attack on whites, Catholics, gays, unsympathetic blacks, the physically challenged—and, most specifically, Jews. Outraged reactions came from all sides, but especially from Jewish and African-American organizations. One Jewish group, B'nai B'rith's Anti-Defamation League, decided to let Khallid's hateful rhetoric speak for itself and published excerpts from the speech in a full-page ad in the *New York Times*. So intense was the reaction to the address that on February 2, 1994, for the first time in history, the United States Senate officially condemned a speech, calling Khallid's words "false, anti-Semitic, racist, divisive, repugnant, and a disservice to all Americans."

Farrakhan's belated response to the outcry, delivered nearly three months after Khallid's speech, only worsened the situation for those targeted in the attack. Although Khallid would be stripped of his duties, Farrakhan announced at a press conference, he would not be excommunicated from the Nation. Nor did he rebuke Khallid himself; rather, he condemned the manner in which Khallid had delivered his speech.

Farrakhan's refusal to censure his minister and his own continued criticism of Jews have made his pronouncements for reconciliation with other ethnic and religious groups seem hollow at best. Of his disputes with Jews, Farrakhan has said, "I would prefer that this whole conflict would go away. But it is like I'm locked now in a struggle."

Although Farrakhan drew intense criticism for

Farrakhan was the prime mover behind the Million Man March, an event designed to demonstrate black men's renewed commitment to self and community. The march, held on October 16, 1995, was the largest gathering of African-American men in the nation's history.

such attitudes toward nonblacks, many African Americans believed he had something valid to say. A few days after Farrakhan's press conference over the Khallid Muhammad affair, the Times Mirror Center for the People and the Press published the results of a survey among African Americans in which 63 percent believed that Farrakhan generally spoke "the truth," and 53 percent thought him an acceptable role model for young blacks. Only a third of those polled believed him to be a "racist or bigot."

Lost amid the controversy swirling around Louis Farrakhan had been his continued commitment to black economic progress. In 1985, Farrakhan again embarked on a nationwide tour, this time to promote his new venture, People Organized and Working for Economic Rebirth, or POWER. The 15-city tour drew little media attention in comparison to the negative publicity that the Nation had drawn the previous year; however, Farrakhan's concept of African-American economic autonomy still appealed to thousands of nonmembers who attended his rallies. During his final tour appearance at Madison Square Garden in New York, Farrakhan was denounced by Governor Mario Cuomo, Mayor Ed Koch, and the Jewish Defense League—but he drew a crowd of 25,000 people.

Having completed his tour of America, Farrakhan launched another, more ambitious crusade— to establish a stable and solid ministry worldwide. Seeking to identify the Nation of Islam as part of a global struggle for human rights, Farrakhan visited the Middle East in 1986. He defied President Ronald Reagan's executive order forbidding Americans to visit Libya—the U.S. government had repeatedly accused the Libyan government of sponsoring terrorism—and met with Muammar Gadhafi, the country's leader and a longtime financial supporter of the Black Muslims. With a $5 million loan from Libya, Farrakhan revived his POWER program and began

a new era in the Nation's effort to realize African-American financial independence.

But he did not stop there. In December 1994, Farrakhan issued a call for African-American men to gather in a massive assembly before the Capitol Building in Washington, D.C. The Million Man March, as he called it, would demonstrate to the country the black man's renewed commitment to himself and his community. African-American men, Farrakhan promised, would "never again be looked at as the criminals, the clowns, the buffoons, the dregs of society."

On October 16, 1995, the country witnessed the largest gathering of African-American men in its

Enclosed in a protective bubble, Farrakhan addresses a crowd of about 10,000 in New York City on "World Day of Atonement," the first anniversary of the Million Man March.

history. Led by Farrakhan, a vast crowd of men from all walks of life converged on the nation's capital for a day of spiritual renewal. In a rare show of solidarity, many black ministers and community leaders who had avoided aligning themselves with the controversial minister agreed to attend. They believed, as Farrakhan stated in his address that day, that "moral and spiritual renewal is a necessity" in a country where black men have a 1 in 24 chance of being murdered, a rate six times higher than that of other Americans; where their life expectancy is that of the white male 40 years ago; where they make up 6 percent of the population but 48 percent of the prison population; where they are twice as likely to be unemployed as a white man; and where 60 percent of black women who give birth are single mothers.

The Million Man March was not without detrac-

Rare glimpses of Farrakhan and his family. Opposite page: with daughter Maria. Below: with son Mustafa (left) after a meeting with South African president Nelson Mandela (right).

tors. Many took issue with the "men only" invitation to Washington. "No march, movement or agenda that defines manhood in the narrowest terms and seeks to make women lesser partners . . . can be considered a positive step," said black activist Angela Davis, a former member of the militant Black Panthers organization. Others, citing the intensity and rage of Black Muslim rhetoric, feared an outbreak of the violence that had plagued the Nation of Islam in the 1970s.

But the Million Man March was peaceful and reflective. In the days following the event, many who attended it described an overwhelming feeling of unity with their "brothers." "The chain was broken," said one black businessman about the civil rights movement during the 1970s and 1980s. "Farrakhan is helping put the chain back together."

On the first anniversary of the Million Man March, Louis Farrakhan commemorated the event with a large rally in New York City, which he billed as a "World Day of Atonement." Acting in that spirit, perhaps, Farrakhan has labored to present a more moderate view of his beliefs and of the Nation of Islam's philosophy and doctrines. Recent surveys show that he has been successful: a 1993 poll by *Time* magazine showed that 73 percent of those surveyed not only were familiar with Farrakhan but also rated him as a more important black leader than South Africa's Nelson Mandela. In recent years, he has also become more personally accessible to the media, appearing on such mainstream television programs as the *Arsenio Hall Show, 20/20,* and *Nightline.*

Farrakhan has gone even further, trying to present himself not as an architect of divisiveness but as a peacemaker. In April 1997, for example, Farrakhan agreed to cancel a planned protest march through the racially tense section of Philadelphia known as Grays Ferry and instead to meet with community leaders for an "ecumenical healing service" in a local church. He appeared with the city's Jewish mayor, Ed Rendell.

Farrakhan closely guards the privacy of his family; thus, very little is known about them. Recently recovered from prostate cancer, he lives with his wife, now known as Khadija, and several of their nine children in the "Palace"—Elijah Muhammad's lavish former residence in Hyde Park. The Farrakhans have 23 grandchildren and are doting great-grandparents of four.

Most people who have met with him privately—including Jews—confirm that the man who publicly rages against the supposed enemies of blacks is surprisingly cordial, soft-spoken, and nonthreatening when encountered face-to-face. This stark contrast between the public and the private man is what makes Louis Farrakhan an enigma to many. Despite—and sometimes because of—his reputation for controversy, Louis Farrakhan remains firmly fixed in the nation's consciousness as a powerful voice for black America.

CHRONOLOGY

———— ❦ ————

1915   Noble Drew Ali establishes the Moorish Temple of America

1917   Marcus Garvey establishes the UNIA in New York

1925   Malcolm X born Malcolm Little in Omaha, Nebraska, on May 19

1929   The New York Stock Exchange crash on October 29 causes millions of Americans to lose their jobs

1931   Elijah Poole joins the Nation of Islam; changes his name to Elijah Muhammad

1933   Wallace Fard appoints Elijah Muhammad chief minister of the Nation of Islam; Louis Farrakhan born Louis Eugene Walcott in New York City on May 11

1938   Mae Clarke and her two sons, Alvan and Louis, move to the Roxbury section of Boston, Massachusetts

1941   The Temple of Islam becomes the Nation of Islam; the FBI begins monitoring the Nation of Islam

1942   Elijah Muhammad arrested and sentenced for draft avoidance and sedition

1946   Elijah Muhammad released from prison; once again assumes leadership of the Nation of Islam

1947   Gene Walcott enrolls in Boston Latin School; transfers the following year to English High School

1948   Gene Walcott begins performing in nightclubs as "The Charmer"; he makes his first television appearance playing the violin on *The Ted Mack Original Amateur Hour*

1949   Malcolm Little converts to the Nation of Islam while in prison; changes his name to Malcolm X

1950   Gene Walcott begins college at Winston-Salem Teachers' College in North Carolina

1953   Walcott drops out of college; marries Betsy Ross in Boston on September 12

1955   Walcott converts to the Nation of Islam and changes his name to Louis X; meets Malcolm X

1957	Louis X is named captain of the Fruit of Islam; appointed minister of Boston temple; Malcolm X leads a crowd of 8,000 protesters to the Harlem precinct to protest police violence against Black Muslim Hinton Johnson
1958	Louis X performs his song "A White Man's Heaven Is a Black Man's Hell" at the annual Savior's Day convention; begins touring with *The Trial* and *Orgena*
1959	"The Hate That Hate Produced" airs on national television
1962	Malcolm X appointed national minister of the Nation of Islam; one Black Muslim is killed and 12 others are wounded in a confrontation with Los Angeles police
1963	Paternity suits are filed against Elijah Muhammad; rift between Muhammad and Malcolm X grows; President John Kennedy is assassinated on November 22; Malcolm X receives a 90-day suspension for his comments on the tragedy
1964	Malcolm X breaks with the Nation of Islam on March 8; Louis X declares him "worthy of death"
1965	Malcolm X is assassinated in New York City on February 21
1968	The FBI charges Louis X and other Black Muslim officials with financial corruption
1971	Nation of Islam erupts in violence as Raymond Sharieff, dissident Black Muslims, and a guard of the Nation's Chicago restaurant are murdered
1972	A clash between New York police and Nation of Islam members results in a full-scale riot; Louis X (now Louis Farrakhan) commended for his attempts to restore peace
1973	Seven Hanafi Muslims are murdered in Washington, D.C.; Philadelphia Black Muslims are convicted of the crimes; New York temple minister James Shabazz is killed; 11 members of the temple are convicted
1975	Elijah Muhammad dies on February 25; Wallace Muhammad is named his successor; Wallace Muhammad removes Louis Farrakhan from his post as head of the Nation's New York temple and relocates him to Chicago
1976	The Nation of Islam becomes the World Community of al-Islam in the West (WCIW)
1978	Louis Farrakhan announces that he is reviving the original Nation of Islam

1981   The new Nation of Islam holds its first Savior's Day on February 26

1984   Jesse Jackson launches his presidential campaign and is supported by Farrakhan, who registers to vote for the first time; both men draw unfavorable attention for their anti-Semitic remarks

1985   Farrakhan unveils his POWER program; tours the country promoting black-run businesses

1986   Farrakhan meets with Libyan leader Muammar Gadhafi to obtain financing for the revived Nation of Islam

1987   Farrakhan renews his POWER program

1993   Farrakhan performs Mendelssohn's Violin Concerto in Winston-Salem, North Carolina

1994   Nation of Islam official Khallid Abdul Muhammad delivers a scathing attack on Jews and other non-blacks; Farrakhan draws sharp criticism for his refusal to condemn his minister

1995   Betty Shabazz, widow of Malcolm X, meets with Louis Farrakhan in New York for the first time in 30 years during a benefit to raise money for Qubilah Shabazz's legal defense; Farrakhan leads the Million Man March in Washington, D.C., on October 16

1996   Calling it a "World Day of Atonement," Farrakhan holds a ceremony commemorating the anniversary of the Million Man March

1997   Louis Farrakhan meets with Philadelphia mayor Ed Rendell in an attempt to restore peace to the racially tense Grays Ferry section of the city

FURTHER READING

Cone, James H. *Martin & Malcolm & America: A Dream or a Nightmare?* New York: Orbis Books, 1991.

Cottman, Michael H. *Million Man March.* New York: Crown Publishers, Inc., 1995.

Halasa, Malu. *Elijah Muhammad: Religious Leader.* New York: Chelsea House, 1990.

Henry, William A. "Pride and Prejudice." *Time* 143 (February 28, 1994): 20–27.

Hull, Mary. *Struggle and Love: 1972–1997.* Philadelphia: Chelsea House Publishers, 1997.

Lacayo, Richard. "Follow the Leader." *Time* 145 (January 30, 1995): 51.

Lawler, Mary. *Marcus Garvey: Black Nationalist Leader.* New York: Chelsea House, 1988.

Lee, Martha F. *The Nation of Islam: An American Millenarian Movement.* New York: Syracuse University Press, 1996.

Levinsohn, Florence Hamlish. *Looking for Farrakhan.* Chicago: Ivan R. Dee, Inc., 1997.

Magida, Arthur J. *Prophet of Rage: A Life of Louis Farrakhan and His Nation.* New York: HarperCollins Publishers, 1996.

Malcolm X and Alex Hailey. *The Autobiography of Malcolm X.* New York: Grove Press, 1965.

Pooley, Eric. "To the Beat of His Drum." *Time* 146 (October 23, 1995): 34–36.

Rummel, Jack. *Malcolm X: Militant Black Leader.* New York: Chelsea House, 1989.

Van Biema, David. "In the Name of the Father." *Time* 145 (January 23, 1995): 38–40.

INDEX

PICTURE CREDITS

THERESE DE ANGELIS holds an M.A. in English Literature from Villanova University and studied rare book cataloging and preservation at Columbia University. She was the contributing editor for Chelsea House's *The Black Muslims* and the WOMEN WRITERS OF ENGLISH series. She is also the author of *Native Americans and the Spanish* in Chelsea House's INDIANS OF NORTH AMERICA series.

NATHAN IRVIN HUGGINS, one of America's leading scholars in the field of black studies, helped select the titles for the BLACK AMERICANS OF ACHIEVEMENT series, for which he also served as senior consulting editor. He was the W. E. B. Du Bois Professor of History and Afro-American Studies at Harvard University and the director of the W. E. B. Du Bois Institute for Afro-American Research at Harvard. He received his doctorate from Harvard in 1962 and returned there as professor in 1980 after teaching at Columbia University, the University of Massachusetts, Lake Forest College, and the California State University, Long Beach. He was the author of four books and dozens of articles, including *Black Odyssey: The Afro-American Ordeal in Slavery*, *The Harlem Renaissance*, and *Slave and Citizen: The Life of Frederick Douglass*, and was associated with the Children's Television Workshop, National Public Radio, the Boston Athenaeum, the Museum of Afro-American History, the Howard Thurman Educational Trust, and Upward Bound. Professor Huggins died in 1989, at the age of 62, in Cambridge, Massachusetts.